MILLION

MOM ENTREPRENEURS SHARE

DOLLAR

SECRETS OF BUILDING BUSINESSES &

MOMS

D1604350

RAISING HIGHLY SUCCESSFUL KIDS

WRITTEN BY

KIANA DANIAL   CHIMENE VAN GUNDY   HOLLY HOMER

BELLA MARSH   ALISON J PRINCE

MAKAYLA PRINCE   OXANA UNGUREANU   NICOLE UNGUREANU

LEANNE WOEHLKE   KATHRYN WOEHLKE

Contents

Praise for *Million Dollar Moms* 1

Preface.. 5

Alison J Prince.. 9

Makayla Prince 37

Oxana Ungureanu 51

Nicole Ungureanu.. 77

Chimene Van Gundy 91

Bella Marsh 113

Kiana Danial.. 133

Leanna Woehlke 155

Kathryn Woehlke... 181

Holly Homer.. 199

Epilogue 219

About the Authors... 223

Praise for **Million Dollar Moms**

"Two years after the birth of my second child, my business was a heartbeat away from broke. Apps sales barely covered monthly running costs and the rest went to daycare. Mom guilt permeated the eight hours between drop-off time and pick-up hour. Outsourcing motherhood wasn't part of the big dream that I had when flushing every waking hour into my business.

With only $237 in my account, I purchased a plane ticket so I could go to a business conference. As I sat in the audience, woman after woman got on stage and shared her story. From single moms to teachers to gym instructors, they all had one thing in common: they did all the "right things" - got the degree, job, mortgage, family - yet found themselves broke. Then they shared how they changed the course of their fate and found financial freedom.

Hearing just one of those inspiring stories gave me enough insight and inspiration to catapult my business into six-figures. Four days later, my business, life and family has changed for generations.

Some of the women who spoke at that conference are in this book as well as others whom I met there. All of these pioneering women believe that impacting women is the heart of their mission.

What I love about the collection of stories you're about to experience is that each one gives you a unique perspective on problems that on the surface seem impossible to overcome. Yet each of these brave women share how they were just like us, struggling to make ends meet, doubting their life choices and having to depend on their own determination to change their fate.

As you turn the pages be prepared to laugh, cry, re-read a passage or sentence, and pause to let the words really sink in. These stories are truly incredible.

As mothers there is one thing that is certain -- every day is unpredictable and children will push you to new limits. The same can be said about entrepreneurship and that is why mothers make such great CEO's. We understand that despite the pitfalls, the journey is so worthwhile.

I'm beyond grateful for the growth in my life as a result of the relationships with the women in this book. They bravely reveal personal and traumatic experiences making it obvious that "they get you." They honestly want to see you succeed. They guide you without patronizing you. They know what you're capable of achieving and clearly show you the path.

Just like when I was sitting in that conference, you are about to embark on a life-changing experience. You will truly grasp that you are not alone and how to write the next chapter of your own story that is both freeing and powerful. And best of all, your story will inspire other women around the world, too.

It's time to be heard!"

- **Carla White**, CEO of Hiro.fm,
  TheGratitudeApp.com, and CarlaWhite.org,
  Host of *Radical Shift* Podcast

"Many women are blessed with the opportunity to step out from behind the desk and embark on a mission to help their own children strive for success. As a Mom myself, I realize that being a parent and an entrepreneur is hard work but we keep charging forward believing in our hearts that we are needed, and the relentless pursuit is worth the sacrifice. I also dream of helping my children learn how to harness the power of turning their passions into paydays, with impact on others being at the core of their pursuit.

One of the best ways to spark inspiration and confidence as a Mompreneur is to hear inspiration-fueled stories of moms who are getting their hands dirty in business, working hard towards financial freedom, and establishing pathways for their children to embrace the possibilities of entrepreneurship, even at a young age.

What I love about the collection of stories within this book is the unearthing narratives from fascinating everyday women about living a life with purpose, being authentic, overcoming obstacles, and pushing towards fulfilled family accomplishments. Oftentimes, hearing heartfelt experiences from inquisitive and optimistic like-minded Moms is what can lift your spirit and remind you that anything is possible with the love of a child.

As you read about these powerful women, be prepared for these stories to stir emotion, cause you to empathize with their struggles, inspire you to take action, and cause you to reevaluate possibilities you could make today that could leave an even greater lasting impression on your children.

Some of the stories will leave you speechless, while others will provide you with educational, actionable, inspiring tips, and ideas for Mompreneurs everywhere. My wish for you is to find comfort, joy, happiness, and fulfillment as you embrace the gift of being a Mompreneur.

Simple stories can make the biggest impact if you open your mind to what's possible. XO"

- **Angie Norris**, "The Stream Queen" and Founder of TVpreneurs Entertainment Network, Author, Coach, Speaker, and Creator of TVStarChallenge.com

Preface

Welcome to a gathering of Million Dollar Moms - Mom entrepreneurs who, in the following pages, will share secrets of building businesses and raising highly successful and service-oriented kids. This group of super-influencers and authors, moms and children, created this volume during ongoing months of uncertainty in the US and around the world. There have been so many "never before in history" events that it is almost overwhelming. Yet, this group of heart-centered, success-and-mission driven entrepreneurs is exceptionally motivated and well-positioned to have a huge impact in a hurry. As moms we want first and foremost to give our children hope, to paint for them a picture of a beautiful world and their place in it. Entrepreneurs focus on solutions so we view the upheaval as an opportunity for change and for good, and we want our children to feel that, too - not in an opportunistic way but in a genuine way. Now, more than ever, people need a way to support themselves and their families that doesn't depend on physically going to a job in which you work for someone else. We see this as a time for expansion knowing that the more we grow our businesses, the more people we can employ which has a ripple effect throughout the economy; as women and moms, we seem to feel the weight of that responsibility to care for others in a huge way. And we certainly believe and accept the privilege of making more to give more. Plus, when we give our children the tools to be intellectually and financially independent, we free them to stand tall and proud and able to confidently overcome barriers. When we follow through on huge dreams, we lead by example so that our children believe they can follow us courageously and enthusiastically. They know we make more money so we donate more to the people and organizations with the most urgent needs. So yes, there is opportunity and hope even in, especially in, the midst of crisis.

We want to help! It is always what drives us. Better yet, we are perfectly positioned TO help! We've already struggled with doubt and overwhelm and come out the other side. We've already been subject to mindset challenges and to being unsure of what to do to help ourselves and others and we've come through to the other side. We've already navigated the logistics of learning what to do first, then next, and the logistics of implementing to get results over theory. And as you'll find as you read this book, we have chosen to be incredibly vulnerable with you so that you know whoever you are, wherever you are, and whatever life has thrown at you, we are certain you will get through to where you've always dreamed of being. We have enough belief to share; you can borrow ours until you've grown your own. We are here for you!

We aren't minimizing fear. We recognize there is real heartache, real loss, and real suffering. The entrepreneurial journey teaches us the long game, just like Motherhood, permitting us to navigate highs and lows, believing with 100% certainty the good times will return and be better than before. In fact, we've already seen kindness multiply and been reminded to reach out more often to our friends, our neighbors, our family, and those who work tirelessly to heal us or keep us safe. We have witnessed shifting priorities and in some ways have come to feel more connected even during such upheaval. And we have become rabid consumers of content while searching for new ways to learn and to earn a living.

The following stories are powerful, transformative, and inspirational. My wish for you is that they nourish your belief, providing you with the courage to keep going in pursuit of your dreams - even if your dreams are forced in a new direction. And if you are still in school - as some of these authors are - I hope you realize the only limits you face are ones you let yourself believe. If they can begin, you can, too! I invite you to discover how collectively we, as these authors demonstrate, may use our unique stories to change the world in small or large measure. Sometimes change is forced upon us. That has certainly been true lately. It can feel hard when we don't choose it; we can use energy to resist or energy to embrace change. Our authors - these moms who wear many hats - are here to help you use this pivotal period in history to build businesses and raise highly successful and service-oriented children!

Alison J Prince

WHAT HAPPENS WHEN YOU MAKE GOD YOUR
BUSINESS PARTNER?

*Alison J Prince is the Founder of 0-100K System, Because I Can Life,
and alisonjprince.com.*

"Because I Can!"

Alison J Prince

Have you ever heard that the way to get financial security is to go to college? Ya, me too. I was told that my entire life and so that's just what I did. I went to college, studied hard, and became a pretty darn good Junior High School Math and Science teacher. I got there early, worked late, and loved what I did. After a month of working I got my first paycheck. I was so excited to have 'made it' financially. As I excitedly ripped open the envelope with my payment stub, out came something that felt more like a slap in the face. I realized that I qualified for government assistance. Now, let me backup. I knew teaching school wasn't going to make me a millionaire, but I thought it would at least allow me to be able to afford my own food.

At the time I was married and had a brand new sweet baby girl. My husband was going to school full time and this government assistance thing wasn't sitting well with me. I decided to get a second job. After about a month of working two jobs, barely seeing my baby, I was completely exhausted. I knew this wasn't the life I wanted to be living in ten years. Heck, I didn't even want to be living that way a year later. So I went to the library in the Junior High where I was working and started reading magazines and books on how people made money. Everything I read pointed to business building. This is where the obsession started. I knew this was it - I knew with this path I could move out of this paycheck-to-paycheck life where we were one broken appliance away from going into debt.

A couple of my friends (Shelley Coates and Missy Smith) and I started talking about starting a blog. We had heard blogging could be a way to start making an income. Between us, we hauled ten kids up to the local Hardee's restaurant where the kids could play in the play center. While the kids played, we plotted out HowDoesShe, our very first website. We each invested $125 which was so hard for us to come up with at the time. All three of us dove into this blog world. We worked hard to gain SEO and gather a following, and I'm pretty sure we worked for negative dollars for quite a while. I was learning a lot about the online world at this time. About a year into it, I realized this wasn't going to pay the bills fast enough, so I went back to the drawing board. I remembered that in blog posts, we'd link people to online stores to buy things that we were using. I started to wonder why we didn't send them to a shop to buy from me. I researched how to start an online store and everything I read said you had to have a bunch of inventory and a big following. Well, I was about to prove that completely wrong.

Now, I realize we had a blog that was starting to gain followers, but I didn't want to disrespect 'my business partners and use that as a means to grow my own site. I decided to start my shop at ground zero. No following. No email. Zilch. I realized that's the best place to start anyway. More to come on how I got customers to my store soon. It's actually one of my secret weapons that I'll share with you. It's so good you don't want to miss it.

Then came the second issue. Inventory. I couldn't afford to buy any inventory, let alone a bunch of it. I looked around my house and I found stuff that was headed to the trash. So yes, my first product was trash. Ya know what? I get emails to this day from my very first customers that say they bought that trash way back then because I didn't sell it as that. What I sold was black sticky paper called vinyl. Now, you can cut it out and make words to put on your wall. But low and behold my cutter was broken, so I couldn't even do that. Instead, I used my trusty ol' scissors and cut it into ten-inch strips. Then I leveraged the power of Pinterest and showed people what they could do with the vinyl. Note: I didn't even have to be creative. Pinterest did it for me. Virtual hug to Pinterest.

Then it was game day -the day I was set to launch my first product out into the world wide web. I clearly remember nursing my baby while I uploaded those first pictures and filled out the description, typing one-handed. I was so scared but so dang determined. I kept thinking that I went to school to be a Junior High School teacher and who was I to be starting this business?

I hit publish on the morning of April 15th, Tax Day, at 7

am MT. Soon after I heard my toddler rumbling upstairs so I walked away from my computer and started the morning/breakfast routine.

I kept hearing a ding come from what I thought was the boys' room and thought it was a random toy. My husband, Jared walked out from around the corner asking what the sound was. Fast. Slow. Fast. Fast. I shrugged it off, I was too busy making breakfast for four hungry kids, and left him to investigate. He came back almost out of breath with excitement and said, "Alison, you are getting sales. Each time that ding goes off it's an order!"

Now, I'm not sure how one body could possibly experience every single emotion in a split second, but that's how it felt. Happy it worked, crying because it worked, worried because I didn't know how to ship, stressed because I still didn't know what I was doing, relieved because I'd worked so hard, mad because I wondered why I hadn't done this sooner, and grateful because I'd heard about others making money online and I wanted to do it, too.

What a rush. I grabbed the baby and toddler and danced around the kitchen screaming loud enough to wake the other two kids. I soon sold out. I made my first $200-$300 in a day selling a product that a few days before was headed to the trash.

I finally figured out how to ship my products later that afternoon and then I looked at my computer and I said, "Oh my gosh, I don't have a product for tomorrow." I went downstairs and rummaged through the bin of leftover birthday supplies and found a gable box; you put cookies in it or prizes for a party.

Perfect! Just what I needed for the next day. Then my husband hollered around the corner, "Let's go camping!" It was Friday, so we loaded up and headed to the campsite, but I was panicking as I still hadn't posted those gable boxes. So I left my husband to set up our tent and I drove around desperately searching for WiFi and found it in the parking lot of a local hotel. The next morning I woke up at the far too early time of 5:00 AM, headed back to the hotel parking lot, and hit publish at 7:00 AM. Nothing sold.

I thought, "Oh, okay. Maybe it's just my connection," and went back to the campground. Sunday morning I went back to the hotel parking lot and published the third item. Nothing sold. I kept hitting refresh. I even drove to the other side of the parking lot, wondering if I wasn't picking up the WiFi signal. I had WiFi but not one sale. I went back to the campsite and said to my husband, "Jared, I just got lucky my first day. It was a one-hit wonder. I'm not cut out for this. I'll pull the site down tomorrow."

At the end of our trip we pulled into our driveway and were pulling out all the muddy, cruddy stuff from camping. I got this strong impression that said, "Alison, I showed you how to do it. Don't stop now."

It was so strong. My husband looked over at me and asked if I was okay. I told him about this feeling that had basically booted me up the backside and he said, "Well, maybe you should listen." It was that night that we decided to make God our business partner. The next morning I got up at 5:00 AM and published at 7:00 AM. And that fourth day we sold out. It was at that moment that I realized that entrepreneurship is a roller coaster ride. I had to get in and sit in that first row and God would lead the way.

My heart was full of gratitude because God knew my plan better than me. I committed to making him my business partner because I knew we could do this together. I showed up again and again, learning step by step. I wasn't blessed with a huge vision of how this business would be built. I was given one small (itty bitty) step at a time.

I eventually sold the extra stuff out of my house and then went to wholesale shops in the States that could ship to me in two to three days. It worked for a bit until I started selling out of their products quickly, too.

Within a few months I knew it was time to start learning how to import. Now, remember my background; I taught 7th and 8th graders. I never took a business class, so hold the snickers… I had to Google what importing meant and how it all worked.

I read online that there was a big conference on how to find products over in China. I called my good friend, Stacy, and said, "Hey, do you want to go to China with me?"

She said, "Nope." The next day I called and asked her again, "Do you want to go to China with me?" Her answer was a quick 'nope.' I'm not known to give up easily so I tried a third time and she said yes. We got on a plane to China, not knowing a word of Chinese and not understanding how to import, but we were wide open to learning. We found manu-factures we wanted to work with and increased the amount of crazy cool products we could sell to dazzle our customers with daily. Each day I posted at 7 am and by year two I had built a multi-million dollar business. Yup, multi-million. I don't take that number lightly because I was used to a school teacher's salary. My brain had a hard time with me saying it because it was such a big number.

I have gone on to sell that first business and today I count my blessings every day. That young mom nine years ago who didn't have any money, lived a chaotic life with four kids, and who was nervous of hitting the publish button, pushed through the fear. I wish I could go back and give her a big ol' hug for taking that first step because she is allowing me to live the life that I get to live today.

I think over the years we start to resist that the uncomfortableness is THE thing that guides us to the life we are meant to live. The more we're willing to walk toward the unfamiliar, the more God is willing to give us. When I started this journey nine years ago, if God told me what I'd be doing today, I would have said, "No way! I can't do that. I'm an introvert. I have way too many kids to do that." I can't spell, I shake when I speak in public, there are a million excuses I could use. But He's guided me step after step and picked me up after I've fallen. I know that the first steps were about moving forward into the unknown and creating a successful business. But it also allowed me to figure out a process and then share that with others. There was a reason why God gave me half a step. Sometimes it wasn't even a full step. It was a half a step. And He's like, "Alison, will you take this half step?" Yeah, I can take that. "Great. Let me give you another step." I do it. "I'm going to give you another step." And He's leading me along this journey. I don't know where it's going, but I trust that He knows my future better than I do. I'm leaning into this uncomfortableness and being okay with making many mistakes along the way.

Hi, my name is Alison J. Prince, and I'm the CEO of alison-jprince.com. I'm a blogger, a podcast host, I coach thousands of others how to start their own online businesses with my program 0-$100K System, and I show others how to live what I call the Because I CAN Life. I've been featured on Forbes and spoken on stage to thousands. I've built four online multi-million dollar businesses and my favorite part is that I'm a wife and mom to four.

Now, I do have to tell you that a few years into this journey of online sales, I had this panic that maybe I was just a 'one-hit-wonder.' I was wondering, "Did I just get lucky in this online store?" So I started another business and built that into a million-dollar business by year two, proving to myself that my process works for me. But I couldn't help but feel that I was given this journey so I could teach others. So I decided to try out my three-step process that I had learned with my 10-and 13-year-old girls. They took the info I gave them and built their first six-figure business - yes, $100K - before they set foot in high school! Now, some have said that I probably helped them. And I try really hard to politely remind those people that my girls did this on their own, as I was running two multi-million dollar businesses (and the blog, which was starting to take off at this point.) The girls had to do it on their own. They needed to see what it took to make this happen. It was my job to step back and let them fly. In the following chapter, you are going to read more details from Makayla, my oldest daughter. She'll even tell you what she wanted to do with all the money. Soon after the success of my daughters, my sister came to me and said, "Hey, can you teach me?" She sold $120,000 in nine months with the same process. Then I had some friends come to me, who were struggling to sell their products at a craft show, and I asked them if I could show them my process. In their first three weeks of doing so, they sold over $35,000.

I felt like practicing my system was proving to me that I was not just a one-hit wonder. The feeling grew that it was my time to help even more people now that I knew others could replicate the process.

Here was the issue, though. I love e-commerce (online shops) because I'm kinda an introvert. I'm happy staying behind the computer screen and letting my products be the hero. So teaching online, putting my face out into the world, something that I knew I was being guided to do, pushed my comfort level clear off the planet earth. But with God's half-step guidance, He led me to find some successful people who were doing things in a way I thought I could model. They were the face of their brand and taught other people without being so 'in your face.' I thought, "Okay, maybe that's something I can do, too." So I launched the 0–$100K System. It's a system that I followed to make my first $100,000 and it's the system that my girls used to generate their first $100,000 - or "$100K." It's the system my sister and my friends followed and hit their $100K successfully, too.

For the last four years, I've been teaching moms how to build a brand, find products and sell them online with this same process. Why? Because they CAN! I'll talk about some of the steps that are in the system below, but one of the really cool things I've discovered is that this isn't just about the money they make. I get to see these women who have become lost in motherhood find themselves again. They discover their passions and learn that they can accomplish goals they had never imagined were possible before they started down this road.

Sure, creating an online business means you're rewarded with pieces of paper with a guy's face on them. But your business can allow you to change your life and your customers' lives and it becomes so much more. This is why I'm so passionate about teaching because I can only personally touch so many lives. BUT if I can help women create more online businesses founded on serving, not selling, they earn money, they learn things about themselves, their confidence grows, and they serve their customers. The money is an important part of it, but all that growing and learning and serving is what gives me chills down my spine when I read about my students' successes.

Three and a half years I think I've been doing this, and we have grown tremendously. And I'm not planning to stop, because these testimonials that come in are proof that more women are discovering who they are and it's lifting everybody up.

So, this is what leads me to what I call the Because I Can Life. I've been to other countries and it can be literally impossible to start a business. Women cannot start a business, and even some men don't have the resources. There was one country we went to where someone had thousands of dollars in their bank account before they even applied for a business license. In our free land, we CAN create a business right from our cell phone.

I think about my grandparents; they didn't have the online world that we have today. They had to mortgage or leverage their house to be able to start their own business. Today, we don't have to. We can look around our home and sell the crap that is collecting dust. I say crap, but it's good crap, right? Someone else's treasure. We can start a business, we can create our own income, we can craft a business around our lifestyles, we can make money to be able to afford our dreams. Heck, we can afford to go pay for our Disneyland trip in full and even buy some of those churros without going into debt!

The "I don't have—" thoughts can come easy, and they can stop us in our tracks. Thoughts like, 'I don't have a big social media following, thousands of dollars to buy inventory, or a creative mind.' Here's my response to that…. Switch your thought to 'I Can.' I can figure out a way to make this work. When we switch our thoughts from 'I don't' to 'I CAN' it starts our journey into what I call the Because I Can Life.

Now, it takes some tools to switch the thoughts to 'I CA.
One of the tools I talk a lot about is Leverage. Yes, leverage.
You become resourceful in your business by finding the things
that can help you to grow. Let's say you don't have 'trash' lying
around your house to sell and start creating income, like I did
with my first product. I get it. But, let's change it into I CAN.
Let me show you how one of my students, Christina, made this
happen. Christina recently moved and didn't have any extra
things lying around her house to sell, so she went to a local second-hand store to sell other people's stuff. Christina worked
out a deal with the owners. She goes to the second-hand store
30 minutes before they close and gets to buy 20 items for $20.
So, each item is a dollar, and every week the store gets $20 and
she gets 20 products to post online. She'll sell each product
anywhere from $25 to $250. That's a pretty good return on
investment, don't you think? She saw what she didn't have and
found a way to leverage other people's stuff to sell. She turned
the 'I don't' into 'I CAN' and figured out a way.

Now, over the years I've seen what selling products online
can do for someone, and the confidence it can give them that
they can achieve goals they set. That's the fun and fluffy feeling,
but there will be times when you post items for sale and you

mments and reviews. Yes, it hurts, but I think

to learn how to deal with the stuff that can

your way. When my daughters were selling in their

shop, Jared and I knew they would occasionally get negative reviews. We taught the girls how to take some reviews with a grain of salt and to use some reviews as valuable feedback and apply it to help build their business. Oh how I remember that awkward teenage phase - in Jr. High I was that girl with the metal-rimmed glasses and braces (aka metal head), and I was scared to talk to anybody and tried to hide a lot. I feel like my girls have been able to grace over the awkward phase because they are learning the good and the bad of how humans can react. They've learned how to communicate, talk down heated conversations, serve customers, and find the good in situations as they've had to dig deep into customer service. Now, of course they are not perfect, but they have been able to learn so much from setting up their own little online store. They are learning the value of hard work, how to be kind online, what dollars are really worth, how to budget, and how to hit deadlines.

Today, I work mostly with moms and a handful of dads because I want parents to prove to themselves (and their children) that they can build a successful online business no matter what start they have in life. The beautiful thing about running an online store is that your family can be involved. For example… wait, before I get started there is a good ending to this story. One time I was selling little girl floral tights. I didn't have any friends at the time who had little girls and I couldn't afford to hire little kid models. So, my toddler boys became the models. Now, before you judge me we took the photos from just above the knee down. When I show them the pictures today, they laugh and say they were glad their little chubby legs were of help. Together we learned how to problem-solve and work with what we had. AND yes, I had to pinky promise with the boys not to show their future girlfriends that picture.

In the early days before I hired shipping out, my kids grew up in a place where they got to help pack, ship, and read the labels. There were times we'd be shipping as a family and a kid would say, "Mom, this one's going to New York City!" And then the little guys would ask, "Where's New York City?" So there would be a geography lesson, right there! Every once in a while, we'd have someone with a famous name come through and we pretended we were shipping to the rich and famous. We had a lot of fun as a family, building and crafting this business around what we were doing. Some kids grow up on a farm, some kids grow up in the city. My kids grew up around brown boxes and packing tape.

That's one of the reasons that I'm constantly talking to moms and dads, encouraging them to teach their kids that they have options. College can be good, but isn't meant for everybody. College shouldn't be a place where you need to get $60,000 in debt to get a degree that will pay you $12 an hour. The weight of that is so heavy. I struggle with some of the student loans they give kids. Here, have one hundred thousand dollars when you're 18! No! Where is the required class that shows them how much interest they'll pay on that and how many years it will take them to pay off?

Why can't we teach our kids how to produce and make money with things they love to do first? How to buy things they want with cash they already have? Instead, the world persuades them to go into debt that they need to pay off over the next 40 years. And only when you retire, can you have fun. That's so backward. I felt I was forced to give set answers in school rather than creatively problem-solve the way I do in my business. The only route offered to me was college, so I took it, but now we can guide our kids to other options.

E-commerce is a way to set up and craft a business that you

love around your life, and yes, I won't sugar coat it. You'll get sick of it every once in a while because that's just life, right? That's why we need breaks and we get to create those breaks because we are the boss. We work hard so that we can have time with our family and afford to live our dream.

I mentioned before some of the steps that I've taught others in the 0-$100K System. One of them is automation. The girls, when they went to school full time, decided to work Tuesday nights and Saturday mornings because Wednesday they wanted to go to a church event and Thursday and Friday they wanted to play with friends. The sales were still being made as they lived their life because your store allows you to take money when you are with friends or, in my girls' case, flirting with the boys at the drinking fountain. You get to craft a business around your schedule. So, for the moms who don't have a ton of time, I get it. You don't need a bajillion hours a week. Yes, it does take work. But you can automate your processes and set up that online cash register so sales can be coming in 24 hours a day, even while you're enjoying time with your family at Disneyland eating those churros.

Now, a lot of people think they need to have big social media followings to be successful at this. I'm going to squash that one real fast. It will take you years to build up an online social media following and you're at the mercy of the algorithm that changes 20 times a year, right? I don't want you waiting that long. So here is where the second step of the 0-$100K System comes in. Leverage influencers - you know, people with big Instagram or FB followings. Influencers have been in this industry for a long time so let them sell your products to their audience. Now, I'm not talking about going after influencers like Taylor Swift. In fact, I don't recommend it. Micro-influencers are the bomb. My secret sauce is to use the smaller influencers. Can we keep that part a secret? Most people go after huge influencers so we can let them do that. The ones under 50-thousand have had amazing results. We've even had some with two- or three-thousand followers that will sell out products in a matter of hours.

Here's the inside scoop on influencers. Influencers are looking for businesses to collaborate with all the time, because that's how they make money. They have something we want - the ability to persuade their followers, and we have something they want - a way for them to make money, and the customer gains because they get an amazing product.

So, you create this three-way win because you're selling, the influencer is making money for their hard work and following that they've been building for years, and then the customer is buying an amazing product.

This is what I call "getting on the jet" of your business. You can walk, heck, maybe it's even crawling, and build your business from zero. But if you're leveraging someone with 2,000 followers, you just jumped on the jet. You bypassed one through 1,999, and your product is in front of 2,000 people very quickly. The influencers send traffic to your store and you make sales.

My girls, when they started, didn't have phones. As their mom, I didn't want them on social media. It was not right at the time. They didn't have a social media following, and they were still able to make over six figures, which is pretty darn cool.

I know so many businesses out there, and they're amazing, but we all have different personalities, right? If you're introverted, you don't want to put your face online; I don't want to be Tony Robbins-level famous. That's not me. Everyone tells me to post more on social media but I don't want to. I want to take that time and go serve the people that invested in me. That fits my personality. I don't have to be uncomfortable. Okay, wait, I do have to be uncomfortable if it serves me and my business if it's about taking the next step forward. But there's also a limit, and I'm not going to be uncomfortable if I don't need to and it isn't serving me.

Then can we talk about the elephant in the room? I get asked this question a lot, almost on a daily basis, so I'm ready with the answer. Here we go. People say, "Alison this sounds so good and I want to start an online store but I don't know what to sell." Have you had that question? Congratulations. You are in good company. Then a lot start to think they need to have a Shark Tank idea - something new and brilliant that nobody else has come up with. And I'll tell you, go watch Shark Tank and you'll see lots of people lose a ton of money. They invest years, their life savings, so much money in a product that nobody wants. The second business that I started after the online store, the one that grew into that million-dollar business, do you know what I sold? Pillowcases. It wasn't anything fancy. But everybody has a pillowcase, right? I didn't have to convince anybody that they needed a pillowcase. You can just sell what's already selling. Yes, that's the third step. Sell what people are already buying. It doesn't need to be hard.

The girls sold scarves to get to their first six figures. How many years have scarves been sold? Forever! The girls just saw the trend, and they rode it. And so, when people think, "I gotta find a Shark Tank idea," I think, "Please don't. You're going to be on a long road and I want you making money faster."

Yes, you can come up with your own unique idea, but first start selling something else to be able to afford all the patenting, trademarking, licensing, and all the stuff that goes into that. Right now, baking stuff is flying off the shelves. People are at home and they want to bake. I'm sitting here with a cinnamon roll in front of me that Makayla made for me last night. Why not sell baking products right now, if that's what people are looking to buy?

Or, outdoor family movie nights are trending because of summer. You can recreate a night at the movies with your family in your backyard. Make it more special than just watching a DVD. That's an opportunity right there. Will customers need popcorn bowls, blankets, striped straws for their root beer? Trending means identifying what people are looking for, and that doesn't have to be a one-time need like face masks. What are people already buying on a consistent basis?

For example, I've got a student named Bev Schweigert. She sells jewelry. Jewelry. She leaned into the step of selling what people are already buying. She's "4Xing" her revenue month over month. Last April, she earned four times my old teacher's salary selling jewelry. It's not easy to do that working for someone else. And then in May, she beat April's numbers. Sell what people are already buying.

We've got another gal, Wendy Kesl, selling glitter. She had a record month in May 2020 - when the world felt like it was crashing. She had big bags of glitter, she was trying to put her orders together, and her daughter walked in and bumped the table. She described it as a big glitter bomb going off. It was a huge mess, right? Have you seen the YouTube videos of glitter bombs? That's what I can imagine. She sat there thinking, "I can't sort this glitter. There's no way."

What they did is they decided to scoop up the glitter and sell these little tiny bottles of a "secret recipe" of glitter combinations. That mistake became her most popular item. Now she has a glitter 'recipe of the month' and people are on a subscription plan with her, excitedly waiting to see what arrives next. Her mistake was her biggest blessing.

She contacted me once, saying, "I'm so afraid I'm gonna fail at this new thing." I said, "I hope you do, because your last failure was actually the thing that made you successful. Now you do something that no one else does, but it's still glitter. You're just marketing it differently." She leans in to her mistakes as her guide now.

One of my students, Kati Evans, found out she qualified for disability. She thought about it for a long time and decided, "I don't want to have to depend on the government." She dug into the 0–$100K System. She found a product - home decor trays - that was trending. In May 2020, less than 18-months from knowing nothing about this business, she crossed the $60,000 mark for the month. She could have taken the easy route and accepted the disability payments. Right? Instead, she dug into all of her insecurities and all of her self-doubts. She went from, "Should I depend on the government?" to "I CAN create a business around my lifestyle and the things I choose to do and I CAN create an income." Her husband quit working and is now able to stay home and help. And here's the fun part. She doesn't post on social media. She is not the face of her brand. She doesn't want to be. She leverages traffic from influencers to help her make sales.

Here's another story. Olive, she's a single mom. A little over a year ago, she had just made a thousand dollars; a thousand dollars was all she'd made over the life of her business. She was about to give up - single mom, thousand dollars total income -

and she was super frustrated. "I don't want to live this life," she said. And she decided to start selling t-shirts. Shirts are not a new idea.

Now, if you do research on t-shirts, it is considered one of the most saturated markets in the entire world. And in month two of running this business, her son was killed in a car accident. She decided to dedicate this business to her son and work through her grief. Now, oh, my goodness, she's at $50,000 a month. She's hired a team and her life is completely changed. Every shirt she sends out, she does it in honor of her son. Her kids work for her. She is one of the most grateful humans on the planet. Her clients feel it and they come back again and again.

Is building a business hard? Sure, life's hard. Sometimes you'll get stressed about shipping or getting orders messed up. But also, you get to enjoy it more as you make the rules. It feels good knowing that you can walk into Target and buy things and not have to say, 'I can't do this.' Or on your kid's birthday, you don't have to say, "I'm sorry we don't have any money." You can have the money to be able to craft the life that you want.

We all want to serve people. That is our heart. That is being human. We have to have money to be able to serve people. Money isn't a bad thing. Money is a good thing, and God wants us to have it because He knows what good we can do with it. He's like, "Please do this." The gals I spoke of above, they are good people. They stepped into the uncomfortable. They didn't crumble when life became hard. They leaned into the fear and found a way to take a tiny step forward.

They stepped into believing 'I CAN.' They leaned into it amidst the chaos and everything else happening in their life. They took a half step, then they took another half step, and now they have the funds and the money that's coming in consistently so that they can serve and live the life they want. Why? Because they can.

I often go back and think about that younger version of me. The one typing one handed, the one with bed-head and in sweats balancing dinner, laundry, and the toddler meltdowns. I'm so grateful for that insecure mom at the time who decided to hit publish.

I wasn't ready when I started. I didn't have money when I started. My life was chaotic with four kids when I started.

BUT...

I did start and NOW I wish I could go back and give my

younger self a big ol' hug because she's allowing me to live the life I have today.

So now I'm going to turn the question on to you. Will your future self be thanking you for starting your 'Because I CAN life' today?

I'll be cheering you on! Why? Because I Can.

Alison J Prince

Makayla Prince

IS SCHOOL REALLY THE PLACE TO LEARN
EVERYTHING?

Makayla Prince is the Owner of Makayla Prince, LLC.
(www.makaylaprince.com)

"Do Something Today That Your Future Self Will Thank You
For."

Sean Patrick Flanery

Hi, my name is Makayla Prince. After speaking on stages and sharing my story with people, they would ask me how they could start selling online. I have put together a course that takes all the complicated information available on the internet and simplifies it, so you can start making money in 10 easy steps! The Miss Boss course teaches you how to sell online without having to build a crazy website, advertise, code, set up an email list, or any of all the other crazy things that you normally have to do when starting a business. It takes you from having no money to making money online and it teaches you how to re-invest the money you make so you are always earning money.

When I was 13 years old, I thought I was living the life; I was having fun! I was sleeping until noon, reading books until 3:00 AM, hanging out with friends whenever I wanted to, and paying my little brothers to do my chores for me.

My parents didn't like that; they knew I had more potential and I was wasting my time. So, they came to my sister, who was acting the same way, and me, and they told us we had three options: we could either move out of the house, do more chores, or start a business.

Being 13, there was no way I was going to move out of the house, and there was no way I would do more chores because I was doing everything I could to get out of chores in the first place. That left me with starting a business. Come to find out my parents knew that we were going to pick starting a business. My mom calls it "parenting," but I say they tricked me into starting a business.

We sat down and had to decide what products we would sell. My mom said, "Okay, every successful business solves a problem. What problem do you want to solve?" I screamed, "World hunger!" at the top of my lungs.

My mom said, "Okay, that's a splendid idea. Let's put that on the shelf and we can address it later. Let's start with something smaller and more manageable and we can work our way there."

So fun fact about me; I always get really cold and so does my mom. Even if it's like 90 degrees outside, we get cold. We decided to find a trendy product that would help with that, and when we looked into it, we found that scarves were trending. We contacted suppliers and influencers and sold scarves. Within our first nine months, we had sold over $100,000. At that age, I had no idea how much money that was.

My mom had to break the money down into babysitting hours. When it clicked, I was excited, and I wanted to go buy all the gumballs in the world because I love gumballs. Instead, with a guiding hand from our parents we put it into a bank account so I could use it for college. My sister and I got paid by the hour working and packing scarves. We had a bit of extra money to play with, but not everything that we had made.

Then high school hit! I joined the marching band during high school. It was intense, but it was so much fun! It meant I didn't have time to run my business the way I wanted to and I didn't have time to get a regular part-time job. I still wanted to work, so I tweaked a few things in my schedule so I still had time to sell products online.

In high school I took a sports medicine class as an extra class to fill in, and I loved it. I told myself that I would become a nurse or paramedic. I had a list of things I wanted to do in the medical field. The class was very hands-on, which is good because that's how I learn the best. We took blood pressure, taped ankles, and more.

I was talking to my teacher, and she said, "You know, you'd be a great nurse." I decided that I would focus on becoming a nurse. That fall, my sister got the flu so we all had to get our flu shots. The nurse poked me and I was on the ground. I passed out from a flu shot! I thought to myself, "Maybe, yeah… maybe not." I couldn't imagine how I could practice on other students (or worse, have them practice on me) so nursing clearly wasn't going to happen.

I wondered about being a physical therapist like my dad, or some other career in the medical field, but I wasn't as passionate about them as I'd been about nursing. I knew that I had a knack for business. So that's what I'm stuck with now, but it's fun and I do love it. I enjoy going to conferences with my mom, meeting amazing people, and hearing stories of what other people have done.

When my parents talked to me about starting a business it was way more appealing than doing more chores so I was in! Suddenly, I was thrown into running a business on top of school and extracurricular activities, so I had to figure it out fast.

As a kid, I had a packed schedule. From 7:30 AM to 2:20 PM, I was at school; then I had marching band practice until 6:00 PM. Once I got home, I had the rest of that time to do homework; however, being the princess I am, I can't function like a normal human being if I stay up past 10:30! I had to prioritize.

When I was in school, I worked Tuesdays and Saturdays on the business. Saturdays were the days I packaged and shipped products. If I had one or two of them come in during the week, I would fill them when the time worked best for me, even if that was not a Tuesday or Saturday.

I made sure I got all my school work done first. If it came down to it, I could pay my brothers or someone else to package and ship orders for me.

I was one of the quietest kids you've ever met, and I just didn't talk to people. So many people didn't know what I was doing. When I got close friends in junior high, I shared with them what I was doing, and they didn't quite understand it but they were excited because I was making money. However, I think they had a hard time wrapping their heads around it because I would get so excited and use all the technical terms - all technobabble - and they did not understand what I was trying to say.

I graduated from high school a year ago and I'm getting ready to start my first year of college (as of when this book went to print.) I took a year off between high school and college to live in Puerto Rico because I didn't want to go to college right away. I am still debating if I want to go to college at all.

I put together a course to help teenagers make money online when they have a busy schedule. That way, they don't have to dedicate hours of time to someone else's business and get paid minimum wage. They can get paid while they are working on homework, studying for tests, or doing the things they want to do to fulfill their dreams. It gives them an opportunity to make money without stressing about a part-time job on top of school.

I'm still brand new at this "selling a course" thing. Initially,

I said that everybody and anybody can join. But I've found that people who are more interested in and already have an idea about running a business are more receptive to what I'm saying and understand the value of what I'm offering. Those who do not understand about business or the technical terms are more hesitant to buy the course and trust me.

I connect with people by taking what I'm thinking and putting it into plain teen language. I haven't gone to school to study business, so I don't know all the confusing technical words, but I've learned some along the way. When I'm creating my ads, I talk about how I'm experiencing the world, and my target audience is able to relate because they are also teens!

Many people ask me, "Why the heck are you going to college? You already know how to do business. Why are you doing it?"

I want to go to college for the social aspect. I know that's kind of weird to say, but I feel that I don't *need* to go to college for a business degree. I already know how to run a success-ful business. I expect to learn the technical terms for what I'm doing and learn how to describe my processes better. I'll also learn how to better keep a schedule, something I have already learned you need to be able to do well.

I'm going to college, but I want to continue my business of teaching teens how they can sell products online without building a website. It's their own business, and they can make more money than if they work for other people, and they can work on their time.

Coming out of high school, I didn't know how to manage my time. It's not something kids are taught, and it's such an important skill no matter what career you end up in. It has always seemed odd to me that it's ignored. Time management would allow high schoolers to free up so much more time in their day to get their homework done and give them space to start their own business if they wanted. It's so frustrating to me that we don't offer that opportunity to kids and instead leave them to figure it out for themselves.

I often talk about my goals and what I want to do in my life. I've always said I wanted to sell a million dollars worth of products, but the reason is so I can take that money, invest it, and use it to change other people's lives.

I was listening to someone speak, and he said, "When you're broke, all you're focusing on is paying the bills and living paycheck to paycheck, and that's all you're stressing about. When you're not worried about money, then you're able to focus on your actual purpose for being here in life and serving other people to your full potential." That's why I want to make money, so I am not stressed about what I need, and I can focus on what other people need and help them.

My friends sometimes come to me and tell me they want to start a business. Then I'll say, "Okay, so you do this and this and this and this," and overwhelm them. I get excited about it because I *know* they can do it, and I have firsthand experience of how owning a business can change your life.

I've learned that I have to teach baby steps, so in my course I say, "Okay, so your first step is you're going to make a hundred bucks here, and then we're just going to set it aside and you can use that to pay for the other things that you will need you to do later." And then I say, "Okay, now you need your legal stuff, and then come back to the business again when that's complete."

I make them take small steps because some of these steps can be scary. Getting a business license and talking to a lawyer can be scary.

Ordering products can be terrifying, too. What if you get the wrong ones? What if you don't receive your products? I congratulate my students as they're progressing and keep supporting them. I tell them, "Wow, you did it. You're making money now. Congratulations! Now go back and do it again faster."

When my sister and I started our scarf business together, we each had separate jobs. She took a lot of the photos for inventory and I did the backend stuff, counting products and making sure everything was updated on the website. Having separate jobs helped a lot, otherwise we would fight. We are teenagers, after all.

Our mom stepped back and let us do it, while offering us tips and tricks along the way. If we were failing, she wouldn't save us. She just let us do what we wanted to do, and if we thought it was a good idea, she'd say, "Here is what other people have done. Here is why this might not work, but this is where it might work. I'm not going to stop you from trying it." That was helpful. We got to do what we wanted and experiment on it by ourselves.

I started working for my mom in high school by doing her social media as a little side job. It was hard because she's my mom, so it would be a little tricky taking her seriously as a boss. We had to find a little bit of balance there.

I know some parents are interested in getting their kids to become entrepreneurs alongside them, but they may be met with resistance. You have to make sure your kids are interested in the business and have a say in it. If you just tell them what to do, it will feel like chores for them, and they will not want to do it.

If you present your kids with options, that gives them a choice and can pique their interest. You might even trick them—or parent them—into picking the right option, just like our parents did!

As soon as you have products available, you can put them online and start making money. This will only work, however, if you are selling the right products.

If nothing is selling, take a step back. Consider your target audience and what they need and want to buy. Think about all the steps you took as you marketed the products. Maybe your pricing was a little off. Maybe the title you used just wasn't as exciting to other people as it was to you. There's so much trial and error.

You are what you're selling and who you're selling it to, so you need to make sure the business fits you. You could put something up on eBay right now and sell it within a week. You could also take six months to build a website and sell products that way. It just depends on what business model is right for you.

My 13-year-old neighbor took my course for teens on how to sell online. It was fun for me to become a mentor and to have her ask questions. The first day she launched, she sold over $200 of her products. She just posted it on her social media and said, "We're doing a sale!" I reposted it and had other people repost it. It was fun to see her succeed.

She went through the entire course and made money. She's only 13, so she doesn't need the money, but now she knows she can do it. I think it's fantastic that as she gets older, she has the confidence to know she can make an online business work if she wants to. She can earn money if she works at it. Maybe she can save enough to buy a car or go to college.

During my senior year, a lot of my friends were thinking about going to college. Toward the middle of the school year, one of my teachers would ask all the seniors, "What are your plans after high school?" Here in Utah, most kids choose either a church mission or college.

If they said they were going to college, he'd say, "What college are you going to?" They would say the college, and he'd ask, "Why?" They would say they wanted to further their education. And again he'd ask, "Why?" They'd reply that they wanted to get a better job. A third time, he'd ask, "Why?" And most often, that answer was to make more money.

I think before anyone jumps into college—I know that often feels like the next logical step—they should take a step back. They should think about why they're going to college and what their purpose is so they're not spending thousands and thousands of dollars getting into debt without being able to pay it off for the next 20 years.

If you're considering college, make sure that is what you need to do before you step into it. There are tons of classes online that you can take. There are masterclasses that you can do that would teach you a lot more and are often more specific than what you'd get in college. College is not for everyone.

If you're interested in learning more about my Miss Boss course, visit my website, https://www.makaylaprince.com/. I also have a free webinar where I teach teens my top three secrets to selling online.

Makayla Prince

Oxana Ungureanu

IS IT POSSIBLE TO FOLLOW YOUR HEART ONE STEP AT A TIME?

Oxana Ungureanu is the Founder and CEO of Trendy Pro.
(trendy-pro.com)

"Follow Your Heart One Step At A Time."

Oxana Ungureanu

(Note: When Covid is over, that's the tattoo I am going to get! It will start on my rib cage, close to my heart, and stop on the top of my feet. This is my permanent reminder to lead with a heart wide open in a fearless pursuit of greatness, making one step at a time!)

I emigrated from Moldova, former Soviet Union, to Canada in 2001. Back home, I had a job as a Head Accountant with KPMG. It was considered a dream job for my Finance degree and I was told I had a great future. I didn't particularly enjoy accounting (I hated it,) so I quit the job the day I found out that our application for immigration to Canada was accepted.

We arrived in Canada with empty pockets and hearts full of excitement about the future; after all, we were in the land of opportunity! We were young and the thought of starting with a clean slate sounded like an exciting challenge. It all started right there at the airport as soon as a smiling Canadian approached us. "What did he say?" I asked my husband quietly.

"I have no idea!" He said firmly, and the deep realization that our English was nearly not good enough hit us like a brick.

A couple of days later, still dazed from the jet-lag, we went on a mission to find a job because we needed money to survive; we went door to door asking for employment. At what felt like the thousandth door I knocked on, I arrived at a restaurant. When I think back, I remember that I was wearing an exquisite fur coat. And I walked into McDonald's asking for a job.

The manager looked me up and down and said, "No." He assumed I was a high-maintenance girl and couldn't do the job. I'd like to say that I was very persuasive and I made him change his mind because my speech was incredibly convincing, but now we both know that my English was pretty bad so I must admit that I broke into tears murmuring something undistinguishable in Russian.

The manager was very confused but he had a good heart so he gave me a chance and he never regretted it! I was running insane hours and I worked nearly every job in that restaurant. I wanted to learn it all! I was fascinated! I could not get enough of the checklists, processes, and automation. I have never seen anything like it! I dreamed of starting my own restaurant one day. Now, looking back, I am glad I didn't!

My next job was at a fabric place downtown. I had to take a bus, a subway and a tram to get to work every day. It would take me three hours there and back but it was all worth it! I used all that time to study Financial Accounting in Canada. I still hated it but I was hopeful that one day I would get back to a corporate job.

I was very diligent about applying for job postings and, finally, it paid off. After what seemed to be a hundred applications, ONE day, ONE person decided to give me ONE chance. He had just started his company and he needed an office manager with a potential to grow. I was beyond myself! I needed that chance!

Isn't it what we all need? Just ONE chance! Just ONE time, when we need it the most?!

I remember shopping for clothes for my first day of office work. Aw, the excitement! I looked so smart!

On the big day, I arrived at the stated address and I was slightly surprised to see that it wasn't an office; it was a house. I rang the bell and a young, confused guy who seemed to have just woken up opened the door. He pointed me to a computer in the living room next to the messy kitchen and left.

"Oh, OK," I thought. "I have a computer, that's good news! Today is my first day at the office and nothing is going to spoil it! Wait! Why is everything in a different language? Oh, no! My Windows was in Czech!" Like I needed a new language to learn!

Time passed; I really liked my job! I liked the guys who were the consultants from the Czech Republic who were helping my new boss kick off his business in Canada. I liked the challenge. I didn't even mind cleaning the kitchen (those boys were messy) or carrying and assembling Ikea furniture when we finally moved to an office. I enjoyed setting up networks and keeping track of expenses. I felt excited and proud that I could contribute to the company that was expanding so fast. As the company grew, my confidence and my responsibilities grew with it; I progressed from a Receptionist to an Office Manager and then to a Finance Manager, overseeing others. It was an IT-based company and I was lucky to be included in meetings so I learned fast!

Right after my maternity leave, I took an assignment for the company's client as a Project Control Officer. Once there I got promoted to an IT Project Manager, and as I gained experience and got certifications I progressed to senior positions.

I had no problem finding contracts that paid well. I was handling complex projects with big budgets and large teams. I took pride in knowing that people wanted to be assigned to my projects. I would spend weekends and evenings researching how to achieve the best productivity, how to motivate the team, and how to activate personal unique capabilities to achieve the best results. As I was gaining more experience, my projects became increasingly more complex because the companies knew I would deliver. And I made it my mission in life to do just that.

I had two kids, Nicole, and Alexis. I was a mom, but I was NOT a dream mom, certainly not every day.

We had a tradition with my kids that every year on their birthdays, I would turn everything off and dedicate the whole day to them. The kids would skip school and we would do whatever they wanted. It started on Nicole's birthday when she turned ten years old.

I wrote different fun activities on paper cards and placed them into a special birthday box. She would pull a card out, read the activity, and her face would light up from the excitement in anticipation for the fun we were going to have together.

We would run around playing Scavenger Hunt, solving riddles, doing tricks on the monkey bars, shopping for toys, making funny faces for selfies and relaxing on the grass pretending the clouds were fluffy unicorns looking down at us.

That was a very special day for both of us and I was a dream mom for one day, once a year, on their birthdays. Then I would go back to my normal life running from one meeting to another, resolving someone else's issues on somebody else's project.

"How many kids' birthdays are there? How many more do I have left before they grow up?" I thought. I treasured them all!

Everything changed on the day my younger daughter, Alexis, turned ten. I see it playing in my mind's eye in slow motion; I can hardly believe I failed so badly that day!

The night before her birthday Alexis could hardly contain

her excitement. She couldn't sleep as she kept asking about the plans for the next day. When she finally fell asleep late, it was with a huge grin on her face. My little sweet girl was growing so fast!

The next day I woke her, hugged her, and handed her a giant balloon that had her first Scavenger Hunt clue written on it. She knew what it meant – her day of fun was just about to begin!

But, sadly, it was not meant to be….

A couple of minutes later I got a phone call from my boss. There was a problem with a project and it had to be resolved immediately! I had to make phone calls, so I asked Alexis to watch TV and wait for me.

It turned into one call after the other, then a meeting, then a conference call.

In the middle of the day, Alexis came to me and said that she was hungry and I told her to wait because I was still on a conference call. She didn't even complain; she just looked at me with her sad eyes full of disappointment and I watched her walk out of the room, looking sad and unhappy.

My heart sank. I wanted to scream. I wanted to quit my job right there… just walk out and never go back.

I didn't! I sat there for a minute swallowing my tears, and then… I dialed in for my next meeting.

That night I fell asleep early because I wanted the day to end. The next day, though, I woke up determined to find a solution that would allow me to live my life on my terms.

The answer did not come in one day; it took some time. My searching was like assembling a puzzle, piece by piece; first I found a glimpse of hope, then a vision, and then at last a clear plan came together as a whole.

It started with Nicole walking into the kitchen and declaring, "We need to start an eComm store!" I didn't know it was the first piece of the puzzle so I didn't think much of it. I said, "You know the rules, baby! Pitch it!"

The "Pitch Rule" became one our family rules awhile back. Every time the kids asked me for anything, I would say, "I don't have enough information to make a decision. You have to investigate, package it for me, and present it in a format that you know will likely guarantee the answer, 'Yes'."

I remember once turning down Nicole's pitch for an expensive iPhone. She announced that she would need 15 minutes of our time in the family board room - a.k.a. our living room. I was watching her fuss over her computer trying to connect it to the TV for the slide show. Once the slide deck was good to go, she disappeared in my closet and came back fully dressed in an outfit suitable for an executive board room. This girl meant business!

Her slides talked about the exciting features of the newest model of iPhone. She finished her presentation with an engaging video commercial, by iPhone, highlighting the features. As the video was running on the living room TV, my eyes were locked on Nicole. She was mesmerized and excited by the device; in her mind she already had it.

The video stopped running and Nicole turned her face to us, her voice shaking from excitement as she asked the question, "Can I have it?"

"No."

Her face turned in an instant; she was about to cry. "Why, Mommy? Why can't I have it? Didn't you see how amazing it was?"

"I did," I said. "I see why YOU would want it, but you didn't give me a single reason why I would want to buy it for you. See, the product is the same – a shiny new iPhone - but the benefits for you (the consumer), and me (your sponsor) are different. So, you need to tailor your message to me, your audience. My answer is "No" but it is not a definite "No." Go back, learn from that video, think of all the objections that I may have, crush them, and return with a perfect pitch.

She got that phone a month later!

With time, the kids became masters of a pitch. Nicole would usually put together a very compelling slide desk and Alexis would read notes from little index cards.

I would often joke that I would go broke if they kept doing it so well. Their pitches were truly irresistible!

And just like that, on Saturday morning, March 18, 2017, Nicole, who was 12, made a perfect pitch that laid the foundation of EVERYTHING that we have now, three years later.

She sat us in front of the TV in the living room and said, "By the end of the year 2017, retail e-commerce sales worldwide will surpass $2.4 trillion US dollars and this is projected to grow to 6.5 trillion US dollars in 2022." Then she declared, "It is time for us to start an e-comm business!"

That was it! We all knew that it was the solution we were looking for!

On March 25th, 2017, we purchased our domain on GoDaddy and created our Shopify store trendy-pro.com. On April 25th we filed our application for trademark TRENDY

PRO. On May 17th, we made our first sale on Amazon.

On August 1st, 2017, I quit my job.

And that's how the story of TRENDY PRO begins... Named by a kid... Inspired by the kids... Designed together with the kids... With a mission to put a smile on a kid's face.

Hi, my name is Oxana Ungureanu, and I am the CEO and Founder of TRENDY PRO.

We are a Canadian company with a mission to support parents in their journey to keep their family active, happy, and healthy. We are just like you - mothers and fathers who want the best for our kids and the family. Our products are designed with love, produced with care, and offered with the desire to put a smile on your face.

Under **the brand** TRENDY PRO we are proud to offer ONLY the highest quality products that we don't hesitate offering to our own kids - toys that children love, family games that we design and enjoy playing, and Fitness Trackers that will get you off the couch and on the move, counting steps.

Under our BeSAFIE Brand we offer personal health & safety products that every family needs to protect what we all treasure the most - the health of our loved ones.

Our customer avatar is a successful, driven mother. Her

name is Susan, she is 40, and she has 2 kids: a 9-year-old boy named Eric and a 12-year-old girl named Amie. Serving Susan and her kids is a joyful and easy process for me because I identify with Susan and other women who have a role to play as loving mothers who also want more from life.

We are curious, we are eager to achieve more, we want to make an impact, we work hard, and we learn fast because our time is limited. We are time-boxed in between kids' drop offs and pickups, executive meetings, presentations, cooking, and singing lullabies.

Often we don't have fancy certifications, but we are the best Agile Project Managers, naturally, because we are constantly juggling priorities. When we fail, we recover fast because there is no time for complaints. A permanent failure is not an option! There is just too much at stake. We have our kids, the Erics and Amie's, the Nicoles and Alexises, who need our financial support and, most importantly, who need our time and attention. They need our hearts wide open for them… listening, speaking in their language and understanding the world THEY live in.

I remember thinking about our first product. Our kids are growing up in a dramatically different world than we did. They love games and technology! What if, instead of expecting our kids to have childhoods like ours, we join them where THEY are and jump into their worlds? That's how we came up with the idea of TRENDY PRO Kids Fitness Tracker that was designed specifically to get the kids moving, set activity goals and track progress in a way kids can relate to.

We didn't just release a Tracker; we designed the process that promotes a healthy lifestyle by gamifying physical activity. It helps the kids and parents stay connected. To achieve that, we designed a colorful Kids and Family Reward chart so that parents can now teach their kids goal setting and tracking and once the kids reach their weekly step count goal, the whole family celebrates together.

We have also released a smartphone app called TrendyFit that allows us to create daily goals, check progress, and send reminders to keep moving. "Gamification" has proven to be a very effective technique because it encourages activity by making it fun for the kids, like a game.

Our first product was an overwhelming success. I couldn't believe what was happening! I kept refreshing my Amazon app, in disbelief, as more and more sales were coming in.

My kids and I were a team, brainstorming ideas, creating, drawing, crafting, and modeling TOGETHER! This was it! The perfect life, the unattainable vision that you see in the movies, but you think you can never achieve yourself. This was my secret dream of being a cool mom come true.

I would like to share what the magic feels like from my daughter's point of view.

Interview with my younger daughter, Alexis (12)

"If you're offered a seat on a rocket ship, don't ask what seat. Just get on." ~ Sheryl Sandberg

Alexis, how does it feel being a part of the magic?

It feels amazing! I feel very involved and, in the moment, when a new idea sparks up in my head, I am always excited to tell my family. I know that no idea is a bad idea and we, together, can turn anything into reality! Building our family brand has changed our lives so much throughout the years! The hard work has really paid off. The thought of being one of the few kids I know with a family business is really awesome. After all, not every kid can say that they get to influence the design and production of toys and games that are enjoyed by thousands of kids all around the world. Not only that, it makes us feel proud as a family to put smiles on their faces when they see

TRENDY PRO arrive in the mail. I remember hearing that one of the customers shared that her grandson's favorite gift for Christmas was a TRENDY PRO Fitness Tracker. That made me think that we are like elves in Santa's workshop. I am proud to be a part of Christmas magic.

Alexis, how was life before TRENDY PRO when mommy had a job?

When my mom was in a full-time job, almost every day was the same for my sister and me. On school days my mom would leave us breakfast on the table and run out of the door early, worried that she would not make it to her train downtown. My mom would work long days during the week. After school, my grandparents would pick my sister and me up from different schools and drive us to their house. My mom would pick us up late - after dark - and we saw that she was exhausted and hungry. On weekends my mom worked overtime a lot, so my sister and I were bored and stuck at home. We had nothing to say about this because this was considered a "normal lifestyle" and we knew that mom was doing the best she could. We really needed a change and we all knew that. Now, my mom is more flexible with her schedule. Instead of working for a boss, my mom is the boss! Not only that, we, together as a family, have learned so much about business! These days my mom is there for me when I come home for my lunch break from school. We enjoy our time together and she is not worried that she is missing something important at work. My mom is more flexible in her schedule now and so much happier than before. We are never going back to the way things were!

Alexis, how does it feel to be the main model of TRENDY PRO?

It's awesome! It's crazy to think that before we had no idea that our lives would change so much. I remember when our mom first announced that we were going to attend a business conference for kids called "Unlock the Secrets" with Russel Brunson, I was so excited to go on a business trip to learn and to meet other successful children. Though I know that I am not as good as my mom, seeing children who are starting their own businesses makes me think that age is just a number and being "a kid" does not mean anything when it comes to business. Seeing other successful kids is really inspiring for me and makes me want to continue learning and taking action.

Alexis, do you know who you want to be when you are older?

To be honest, I would like to see where this business takes us. I am very inspired by my mom and if I ever need help, I can always count on her to help me find the answers in life. I am still searching and if I see something that moves me or makes me think, "Wow! Other people might love this as much as I do!" then my job as an entrepreneur would be to bring it to them. My goal in life is to bring joy to the world whether it is to kids, adults or anyone of any age. I would like to be able to contribute and do good for the world. I am considering Psychology as my college degree as I am fascinated by nature and the world around me. This may not necessarily turn onto a job in the future but I would like to study so that I can share it with the world. Oxana - & Alexis

The success of the first release inspired us to keep designing and producing more.

The family brainstormed what would make a great next product. We all agreed that it had to align with our company mission and it must bring joy to our customers, encourage physical activity, and complement our main product — TRENDY PRO Kids Fitness Tracker.

We decided to create a Scavenger Hunt Game with Walkie Talkies. We understood that kids love pretend play. We thought, "Why don't we leverage this to promote imagination, creativity and physical activity by engaging kids in a Spy game, where everyone's a Hero on a mission to save the World?"

In the game we designed, the players become a part of the imaginary spy environment, taking turns playing as Spy Master, Mission and Base Leader. The kids learn coding and decoding in spy language, communicating over 2-way radios, observing surroundings while looking for Scavenger Hunt objects indoors or outside.

I must admit, I was very nervous about releasing this game. I have organized multiple Scavenger Hunt and Treasure hunt games for my kids and they always had a blast - but designing a game for thousands of kids across the globe? I had my doubts! Could I really do it? I am not a designer, not an engineer, and I didn't know if other kids enjoy the game as much as my kids did.

When the production of 2,500 units was complete, I didn't have the courage to launch it. Only six months later after I hired my brilliant Operations Business Manager, Gwenn, did the game get a fair chance. It took off like fire!

Gwenn turned out to be the most amazing manager for our staff and also the person I needed the most. She gave me the courage to keep creating and designing because from that point on I knew I could!

The next enhanced release of the Scavenger Hunt game is currently in production and expected to be available on Amazon in the US, Canada, UK, Germany, Spain, Italy, and France by the time this book is published.

We are also taking our Fitness Trackers to a totally new level. Our next release is called **TRENDY PRO** Fitness Tracker, Trendy Pup edition. It is scheduled for launch when the kids are ready to go back to school. We will offer an upgraded colorful and feature-rich model that will come in bright packaging. Inspired by the iPhone unpacking experience, we have designed the box to offer an exciting surprise as kids unwrap their gift.

The giftset will include a cute glow-in-the-dark puppy toy named Trendy Pup, who will become their fitness and life pal. In addition, the kids will be able to customize their bands.

I wanted this edition to be especially thoughtful, colorful, and loving. Spring and early Summer, 2020, were hard on all of us, especially kids who had to witness the whole world turn with Covid. For many, this was a period of sadness, insecurity, and isolation as the schools closed for quarantine.

Designing the new release during quarantine, I couldn't help but think that now more than ever, the kids needed our support, positive thinking, bright colors, and happiness. Most importantly, during such uncertainty they need to know that they are not alone.

That's why our new release will include Trendy Pup, a little toy that will brighten their room in the dark and be there for them when they feel lonely. Trendy Pup edition will also mark our first release of a children's book, written by Alexis and illustrated by Nicole. The book is going to be about a magical place called Trendy land. This is the place where Trendy Pup came from because he had heard a call of a lonely child.

As devastating as Covid is, it is also a blessing that has allowed families to slow down, re-connect, and appreciate what matters the most. It helped us treasure each other a little more; it reminded us that every day is a gift that must not be wasted. It also made us appreciate the ability to work from home plus appreciate mentors who inspired and guided us on the path.

Looking back, I had three especially influential mentors

who shaped my vision: the first - tactically, the second - strategically, and the third - mentally. Without them, I would not be writing this story, so I must acknowledge them for my story to be complete.

Kevin David grabbed my attention instantly the minute I saw him on the screen. It wasn't his young handsome appearance that appealed to me; it was his determination to succeed wrapped with his commitment to do whatever it takes. Coming from a similar finance background, Kevin spoke my language of numbers and analytics that made me believe that the success in this business is not as unpredictable as it seems. It may seem odd now considering Kevin's exposure, but back at the time he was a little shy and very simple. The free YouTube video that he shot in the kitchen of his small apartment, with a box of Cheerios in the background, was my first serious exposure to the Amazon FBA business model that changed my life.

So when Kevin opened the shopping cart for his first Black Belt training I didn't hesitate. I bought a red vinyl binder and printed every single module of his training, highlighting the important topics and separating sections with colorful index cards.

Kevin's training gave me the tactical knowledge and operational guidance that simplified the execution. His Facebook group gave me something indefinitely more valuable that I will treasure forever – it gave me friends I love and a community I can always lean on.

My second mentor, who had an incredible impact on my business strategy, was **Ryan Daniel Moran**. He is just brilliant! He guides with his heart wide open and he is never boring! I came across one of his presentations on YouTube as I was getting ready for my first product launch and, to this day, I follow everything he says. One of the main concepts he shared is very relevant to this book:

"If you have three to five products, at an average price point of $30 per unit each, and you sell twenty-five to thirty units per day, you have a million dollar business."

It is that simple! I remember so vividly the first time I heard this from Ryan! I took a calculator and I wrote the numbers down. I stared at my notepad letting it all sink in. Suddenly, all my overwhelm went away because I knew I had a simple formula to follow and I could do it! Ryan gave me permission to drop the complexities of the digital marketing that I hadn't yet mastered and helped me focus on something I could do right away, one product at a time. This was his simple formula:

Product research => Product development => Production => Release => Celebrate!!! => Repeat until $1 Million Revenue is achieved

I did just that! I did not manage to turn it all around in twelve months, as he said was possible. But….

I hit my first Million in 18 months!

So if you are discouraged or overwhelmed, you don't know what to focus on, or you don't know where to start, I highly suggest a book by Ryan that he has just published. It is called *"12 Months to $1 Million"* and you should get it now! Once Corona madness is over, the first thing that I am going to do is fly over to Austin to get my copy signed by Ryan.

My third mentor's name is **Russell Brunson**. I love him and everything he does and the people he attracts! I remember attending my first Funnel Hacking Live conference in 2019. I arrived at the most gorgeous venue. I looked around and saw unfamiliar faces, people hugging, and everybody lining up at massive doors leading to the conference hall. The excitement and suspense were palpable! The doors opened all at once, the music filled the room, and people ran in as if their life depended on it!

What. Is. Going. On? What kind of business conference is that?

I found myself diving deeper and deeper into the world of ecommerce and digital marketing, one presentation after another. I felt like I was on a different planet, or maybe in a parallel universe, looking at beings with supernatural abilities; they lived in tribes, told people inspiring stories, and built 'epiphany bridges.' They possessed a deep knowledge on a variety of topics and everything seemed to be a "secret" that they couldn't wait to share. Their stories would always start with a "Hook" which was extremely alarming initially, but then I realized that these people were safe and very giving. Their language was very confusing as the words sounded like English - "Funnels," "Offers," "Waffle" or "Pixel" - but with unfamiliar meanings. It all sounded so strange and magical that I fully expected some colorful unicorns to come out flying around and sprinkling some pixie dust.

Come to think of it, there was a Unicorn on stage!

It was Russell and he came on stage surrounded by flashing light, loud music, and people cheering. He told stories, showed doodles on the big screen, and talked about frameworks and funnels; but most importantly, he introduced me to the speakers who later became my dear friends. Their stories touched my heart and made me cry and laugh reliving their failures and rise to greatness. They made me believe that ANYTHING is possible; you just have to start somewhere, make your first step into the unknown, and never look back because things will never be the same.

Russell Brunson is the reason I am writing this book. He likes telling the story of Roger Bannister who broke the 4-minute mile on May 6, 1954. "Prior to that, everyone thought it was impossible, and after Roger broke it, proving it was possible, many people since then have been able to do it.

Two years ago, Ryan Danial Moran broke my limiting belief and today I want to break yours.

If I was able to succeed as a single mother with two kids, in an unfamiliar country, with broken English, and no sales or marketing experience, don't you think you have a higher chance for success?

Don't waste it! I am proud of you!

I am telling this to you and to the younger version of myself, an innocent girl who arrived in this land of opportunity not so long ago, looking at the world with her eyes wide open, searching and hoping for a miracle, when in reality, the miracle was within, all along.

YOU are the miracle!

So, if you hear the calling, you must follow your heart! Create, contribute, teach others, lead with your heart wide open, and together we rise...

One. Step. At a Time.

Oxana

Nicole Ungureanu

IS AGE JUST A NUMBER?

Nicole Ungureanu is the Owner of the designer brand Annicko. (Annicko.com)

"If you want to achieve success, all you need to do is find a way to model those who have already succeeded."

Tony Robbins

When I was younger, people always told me about the traditional life path: good grades will make you successful; school is always your priority; your job defines you and determines if people will be proud of you; and making money is the only key to being happy.

I remember very vividly when I was in elementary school, my mom always waking my sister and me extra early. We wouldn't have time to eat breakfast together - just a quick sandwich and we'd be out the door. I remember telling my mom "good morning" and her barely hearing me because she was busy making sure she didn't forget anything for work. I remember missing her and wishing I could have just an extra minute with her before work. I remember wondering, "Will this be me in 20 years? Not spending any time with my kids, working every day till it's dark? Is this what 'working hard' will look like?"

When we're young, we're always told to prepare for the future. Constantly, we have the irking feeling in the back of our mind so that we wonder if everything we do is somehow going to impact our futures. I remember hearing about a study on CTV news that was done by the Toronto District School board which stated that 73% of students aged 14-18 reported that they worried about their future and felt huge pressure to achieve good grades. "You feel this huge weight. There's so much pressure on you to succeed and get a good grade," a female student said.

But what if I told you that life can be more than worrying about your future, constantly working, and fearing you are not enough?

The day it hit me....

I woke up one Saturday morning, relieved and overjoyed that it was the weekend. Absolutely no school, free time, but most importantly, breakfast with Mom. I had spent the morning watching YouTube videos about crafts and baking. Suddenly, a video appeared in my "recommended folder," a video of someone explaining how you can make money by selling products online. I was taken aback, captivated, and impressed. I used to play with my sister, pretending to have a store, using paper with numbers written on it as money. We would take turns being the store owner, always excited when it was finally our turn. I saw this video and I knew exactly what I wanted to do. I was so excited to share my bright idea with my mom! I said, "Mommy, why don't we open an online store? We can sell all sorts of products to online customers! It's super easy!" Although at the time I really didn't know if it was going to work, I knew this was my chance to have my dream come true! I could have my very own online store.

It seemed as if the world was moving in slow motion as I waited for my mom's answer. Is she going to say yes? Finally, she said, "That sounds like a great idea!" I was ecstatic! "But...."

she said, "You need to do some research before we can do anything."

I got out my computer and spent the entire day researching how to start an online store. I was so excited to be a part of something completely different. I learned about domain names and drop shipping. But most importantly, I was excited that my mom and I found something we could do together and were both passionate about. My mom said, "You know, in a real company, you never just ask the boss for things you want. You have to pitch it to him or her with all of your research ready and explain why you deserve the things you want." I realized that if I wanted to start this online store with my mom, I would need to learn how to properly pitch the idea to her. I was nervous to present my ideas to my family, but I knew that I had to be passionate and confident in my research in order to wow my family and produce the same type of excitement in their eyes as I had in mine. By the end of my pitch, I could see by my mom's proud face that she was just as excited as I was!

At this moment, I knew I was on to something and that we were going to create something extraordinary.

Feeling the Creativity Flow....

Before we could start our online store we had to decide on a product. We knew we wanted to do something with kids because our plan was always to fill kids with the same spark of magic and passion as we felt when we first decided to start our company.

At the time I was begging my mom for a fitness tracker. All the cool kids had it and I wanted to have the cool new gadget everyone was raving about. The only problem was that they were extremely expensive and not designed for kids. They were big and hard to understand and that's when it hit us. We needed to do fitness trackers as our first product! We knew it was the right product for us because we began treating it as our baby, constantly thinking of ways we could make it perfect for kids. One day my mom said, "Nicole, we need to make sure that the instructions are super easy to understand for kids." My passion lies with making creative things art-related. I also love absolutely anything to do with media and cinematography. So I thought, "We should make a fun instructional video for kids!" We knew that in order for our product to stand out from all of the others, we would need to make sure that it was completely different. We began brainstorming on how we could turn this simple fitness tracker into something extraordinary.

My sister and I got to work, creating an in-depth script. We made sure to explain the instructions and features of our fitness tracker in the easiest and most interesting way in order for small kids to be able to follow along and not get confused. As kids, we felt that we had a responsibility to make sure our product was the perfect fitness tracker for children. We had a special superpower, the power of being kids ourselves! We knew exactly what would stand out and what would be attractive for kids. Working together as a family we designed something out of this world!

I was excited to begin the filming portion as my sister and I love being in front of cameras. I remember looking outside of our patio and seeing the beautiful blue skies, milky fluffy clouds, and the greenest branchy trees. And I thought to myself, what a beautiful day to make magic happen.

We sat outside in the cool breeze and set up our baby (our fitness tracker) on the table and I was so excited to set out all of the beautiful band colours we chose for our product. Finally, we could see our product coming to life, with a real video now advertising something that had been just a thought or a dream for so long. We asked our mom to hold the camera as we began rehearsing our lines, and I could see in her eyes that she felt the very same feeling as I did; all of our work was finally paying off.

That video is still one of our most treasured marketing videos because of the happiness we felt to be so close as a family and the proud feeling we had knowing that our product was one day going to be more than just about making money.

Inspiration Everywhere....

As much as we like to believe that wishing for something will magically make it come true, the truth is that sometimes we need a little push to show us exactly what we are truly capable of.

In the summer of 2019, my mom decided that it was finally the time for us to go and see Russell Brunson on stage. He had been an inspiration for her for so long and she thought it was finally our turn to see exactly what made my mom so passionate for E-commerce. We hopped on a plane and flew to Denver, Colorado where our lives would change forever.

Russell Brunson was holding a special event called the 2CCX Unlock the Secrets for kids. And just like we made sure that our fitness tracker was easy to understand for kids, Russell tailored his business presentations in order for the young audience to follow along and understand. It was a fancy business event with successful and talented people, and I felt slightly small compared to the rest of the amazing people attending the event. I thought, "They are capable of much more than I am, I am not as good as they are, and how am I supposed to do this? I'm just a kid." Suddenly, Russell Brunson welcomed Makayla Prince on stage, a young girl who explained how she started her own business all on her own. Finally, I felt a spark go off in my head! If she could do it, so could I! (And now we are in a book together!)

I finally got that push I needed, a perfect vision of what I wanted to do and be in the future. It was so clear to me; I can do anything. Just because I am a kid doesn't mean I can't start now to create my dream. I turned my head to my mom and said, "I want to be just like that."

Of course, my mom was extremely excited for me and super supportive. She told me that it was just the fourth quarter and that it was the perfect time for me to create my own product! But although I had the confidence and push to create my own business, I still needed guidance and money. It was difficult to start a company at my age but knowing that my mom was by my side, someone who had already experienced creating a product, I knew I would have help if I messed up, and that I could trust her no matter what.

I researched possible products and we decided on a hand-controlled mini toy Drone. Again, we wanted to do something with young kids as that was our favorite audience to work with. We loved this new product idea because a remote control was not needed and very young kids could play with it. It was able to sense your hand underneath and fly upwards, spin, and do tricks! I was so excited to sell a product that was something new and my very own.

But even though it was an exciting product, I knew it would still take a lot of work in order to turn this simple Drone into something outstanding.

I worked with our representative in China in order to find the perfect Drone as our product. It took a couple of proto-types but after a while we found a Drone that was exactly what we envisioned for our company. I handled the process choosing the correct specifications and finally purchased 5,000 units. And although it might seem like most of the work was behind me, the scariest part was still ahead. We had manufactured thousands of dollars of toys for kids; the moment of truth was seeing if we would be able to sell them.

Unique Offer....

At breakfast, my mom explained how we had 5,000 Drones quite similar to others available on Amazon. At Trendy-Pro, we don't just produce things that everyone else produces; that's not what we do. We take things and make them bigger and into something extraordinary.

I wondered how we would make our Drones stand out and what would make our customers choose our Drone over someone else's. These are all things that are important to think about and one of the key things that we learned from Russell Brunson and Mikayla Prince.

We decided that our Drone was going to be UFO-themed and UFO-shaped. We intentionally framed our product in a way that would spark creative and amazing ideas for the kids who use our products. It quickly shifted from children playing with a toy to children coming up with pretend stories and playing with a real-life alien UFO!

But we still needed more to really put our product on a pedestal, high above the other Drone products on Amazon. We asked ourselves what was interesting about our mini drone:

How does it fly? How does it work? We decided that these were the questions that kids would ask, too. Providing the context that answered those questions is what would truly make our product outstanding!

I researched some information for the kids on how the drone worked as well as names for the key components of the Drone. I explained these things using simple terms to make sure young kids could understand. But we also wanted to make sure that we were teaching the kids something valuable. We came up with an Activity Book to include with the product. It includes a word search, hand drawn UFO-like pictures for coloring, and informative facts about Drones. It was exciting to create something purely for kids to have fun and enjoy our product even more.

My mom came to me one day and said, "We're finishing manufacturing the product today. You'll need to create the activity book by the end of the day." "But how?" I asked myself. "I have school and homework. How am I supposed to create an activity book from scratch so quickly?" I began feeling worried that maybe I wouldn't be able to do it. My mom said, "Don't worry about school; this is much more important. In the long run, you will learn more from this business assignment than from your homework. Stay home today and work on your business." I felt a huge pressure lifted off of my shoulders and I was able to focus on something that I was really passionate about.

I spent the entire day working on the Activity Book. I made a word search from scratch, and I drew by hand UFOs with Aliens in order to spark some creativity and fun for the kids. I finally finished all of my research in order for the kids to learn how drones are able to fly and sense your hand. I finally felt the end goal was coming closer. I was about to have my very own product!

I am pleased to say by the end of the first eight weeks, Trendy-Zip made more than $150,000 in sales!

Model For Success....

The success of my first product proves that there is more to life than your grades in school. Grades do not define you or your future. Know that anything is possible. As a straight-A student, I used to feel weak and worthless when I did poorly on a test or quiz. I want you to know that you don't have to rely on your grades to be happy. Find something you are passionate about and watch as your passion grows wings and lifts you off the ground.

I have always loved the quote by Tony Robbins that begins this chapter, "If you want to achieve success, all you need to do is find a way to model those who have already succeeded."

If I can create a business at the age of 15, and my mom can create a million-dollar company from nothing but a dream, you can too!

Nicole

Chimene Van Gundy

WHEN YOU HIT ROCK BOTTOM, WHERE ELSE CAN YOU GO BUT UP?

Chimene Van Gundy is the President and Founder of Outstanding Real Estate Solutions and the Founder of Mobile Home Millions (mobilehomemillions.com)

As a child, I never felt like I had a safe home or that I fit in anywhere. I'm the fifth of seven children—my mom had seven kids in ten years! I grew up in Des Moines, Iowa, on the east side. My dad worked for Firestone and my mom stayed home; we were very poor. My parents had a bedroom and the seven kids shared two bedrooms between us. All nine of us shared just one bathroom. All my clothes were hand-me-downs, and I don't think we owned a TV until I was about eight. I have an older brother and sister and another older brother and sister that are twins. I have four siblings born before me, and two after me, including the baby of the family, so I suffered from middle child syndrome my entire life.

I was often ignored and very neglected growing up. More than once, the family would get home and only then realize they had forgotten me and left me. I was left at numerous restaurants by myself. My dad would have to turn around and come back and get me because they forgot me again. We were raised in a church cult which, as you might imagine, caused a lot of trauma and psychological damage. As a young child I was also horrifically sexually abused. In my teen years, I was thrust into the foster care system even though my other six siblings remained at home. I was sex-trafficked up and down the Chattanooga, Tennessee to Dalton, Georgia corridor in the foster care system.

I became emancipated when I was 17 ½ years old. I was the first in my family to go to college. I graduated with honors with a BA degree in Criminal Justice from the University of Texas at San Antonio, the first in my family to earn a college degree.

I followed the traditional trajectory. I got married and had four children. After 14 years I divorced, stayed single for about 18 months, and then met my current husband. He had no children of his own at the time and took me on as a package deal—me plus three (as my oldest was already an adult.) We had one more child together so I am mom to five!

When we married, we moved from San Antonio, Texas, where my then oldest child, Bella, had grown up, to New Braunfels, Texas. It was a hard move for all my kids, being pulled away from their friends, but it was especially hard on Bella since she was 13. She was so angry with me—mad about her dad, mad about the move.

But I had to focus on work because my children were my responsibility. I was the Director of Case Management for the Women's Shelter in New Braunfels, helping women who were facing domestic violence issues. To make more money, I moved over to the for-profit corporate world.

Eighteen months later, in February 2015, I was laid off without warning. I had no idea what I was going to do. At that point my marriage was not even two years old, and I was terrified my husband would leave me. I remember sitting in my car in the parking lot at work crying after being escorted out of the building by security. I was so angry and felt so betrayed! I had worked hard, grown the division, and made them money. Then one day with no warning I was redundant. It was the most inhumane slap in the face that you could ever have in your life.

I remember I went home, I cooked dinner, I got the girls to bed, and then I went into my bedroom and I just started crying.

My husband asked what was wrong. I told him I was sick and tired of working for non-profit agencies and corporations, giving them everything to make THEM a ton of money. They didn't value the people OR appreciate the work. I told him I'd make my own money and figure it out.

Because I had a degree in criminal justice with a minor in law and a minor in sociology, I was a paralegal and a notary. I used those skills to freelance and made $200–$600 per day but the income wasn't predictable. That was when a friend asked me if I'd read *Rich Dad, Poor Dad* by Robert Kiyosaki. When I read it, I was blown away.

Growing up, we never had enough money. My family was all about scarcity; my dad even sold his vacation days so that there would be enough food for seven children. But when I read that book, I had a real epiphany about money. All my false beliefs were shut down with that book. I became obsessed with learning about money, and I found out that Kim Kiyosaki, Robert Kiyosaki's wife, taught women to be financially independent.

I attended her free event, and she cited statistics that women who divorce experience a disproportionate decline in household income and standard of living with a sharp increase in the risk of poverty. Divorced women also face a higher risk of losing homeownership, and their responsibilities as single parents impede their economic recovery. I had seen this play out in my life, so it resonated with me.

Nicole De'Ambrosia, who had appeared on *The Apprentice*, was also at Kim's event. There was a drawing for a three-day real estate boot camp over Mother's Day.

I won! I was so excited!

I learned about "the Rule of 72," the "four buckets of money," and how the bank doesn't want your property. I was just blown away. I remember thinking I was sick and tired of depending on my ex-husband to pay child support and worrying about whether I could feed my babies.

I didn't think it was my new husband's responsibility to pay for the kids I brought into the marriage. I knew on that day, if I did not decide to change something, that my life would be like the definition of insanity: Doing the same thing over and over again while expecting a different result.

At the end of the three days, it was my turn to meet with

the success team. They told me the cost to work with them was $20,000. I was sticker shocked, but what I asked was, "Can you guys hold this price for seven days?" They said they could.

I went home and knew I had hit rock bottom. I sold some Thomas Kincaid paintings, a collection of Precious Moments, and some jewelry. I came up with $17,000, and my husband loaned me the balance. That's how I launched.

My mentor came to Texas in July 2015, and from July to September, I did exactly what they told me to do. I made $180,000 and paid off all my consumer debt. And then, at the end of September, our house caught on fire. My husband and four kids were fine, but our entire life was disrupted.

In 2016 I relaunched my business and I haven't looked back since.

We all need food, water, and shelter. In terms of shelter, I realized that manufactured housing is the last affordable source of housing in America. I never want anyone to not have a home to live in because I remember what it was like to not have a safe place to call my home.

Most real estate investors overlook mobile homes—manufactured housing—referring to people who purchase them as "trailer trash."

I quickly staked my flag in the industry. In fact, I've now been on PBS's *American Health Journal*, hosted by Roger Cooper, talking about the psychological, emotional, and mental benefits for seniors living in mobile home parks versus living in nursing homes. As this book goes to print, I'm filming a documentary with PBS on affordable housing in America.

Since getting started from 2015 to now in mid-2020, I have fixed and flipped over 776 mobile home units. In 2017, we went international, working in Ireland, New Zealand, Australia, and more, where manufactured houses are referred to as "holiday homes." I left the non-profit and the corporate sectors to provide quality, affordable housing to people, and it's the best feeling in the world!

Hi, my name is Chimene Van Gundy, and I'm a real estate investor and entrepreneur with Outstanding Real Estate Solutions, Inc. and Mobile Home Millions, LLC.

I invest in mobile homes and mobile home parks, providing affordable housing to people across the U.S. I'm known as "the mobile home millionaire" because I have fixed, flipped, and wholesaled close to 800 units in five years. I also have an educational company where I teach people how to make money with mobile homes.

I'm proud that I've been honored with a Lifetime Achievement Award and will be celebrated as Woman of the Year for 2020 by P.O.W.E.R. (Professional Organization of Women of Excellence Recognized) for outstanding contributions and achievements in the real estate industry and investments. I am also the Mentor of the Year for 2020 by P.O.W.E.R

I manage five companies and I'm able to do so in part because my oldest child, Bella, works with me. She was still angry, but what saved our relationship was my example. I think she saw her mom not settling for a poor relationship, making it happen with business, and living out her dreams.

Now she knows she can, too, because she saw me do it.

And now you are reading a book I've co-authored and maybe something in here will change your life, just like mine changed! Think about this: If you make a man a millionaire, you make him a millionaire for life, but if you make a woman a millionaire, you change five generations of families!

I have now changed the next five generations in my family for all of my children. And it started with me; I'm a pioneer. That's hard to come to terms with, but also it's amazing! Sometimes when I think about my childhood, I feel like I'm living in a dream because I just can't believe this is my life now.

Bella and I have reconnected and we're extremely close. She is like a "mini-me" and I'm very proud of the young woman that she's become. She's gone through a lot of adversity in recent years and she came through stronger. Bella handles all my webinars, strategy, tech support—everything to do with Mobile Home Millions. She's also helping me launch a podcast that will run by the time you read this called *Positively Charged Women: Positively Charge Your Life Financially, Spiritually, and Physically.*

Additionally, I am launching a Women in Leadership group with high-level coaching for women. I want women to know they don't have to ask permission to take charge of their life. And the other thing is that nobody is coaching mothers and daughters... Nobody!

Bella and I are working on a platform to coach women and their daughters, almost a female version of Garrett J White's "Wake Up Warrior." I see a huge generational gap with mothers and daughters. Real estate and investing are both male-dominated fields and we want to change that and make it completely accessible to women.

For anyone wondering how they can do what I have done, here are some pointers. For starters, I recommend everybody read *Rich Dad, Poor Dad* by Robert Kiyosaki. Next, watch *The Secret*. It's an amazing show about the law of attraction. Do the things they tell you to do. I made my dream board, and I took a one-dollar bill and wrote seven zeros with two commas to turn it into a $1 million bill and I hung it up on my ceiling. It was what I saw every morning and night.

Start listening to podcasts like *Radical Shift* with Carla White, *InFLOW* with Michelle Bosch, my podcast, *Positively Charged Women*, and other podcasts that uplift women.

You cannot do anything unless you change your mindset. You need to tell yourself positive affirmations every single day. And then you take those steps to do it. I redid my entire schedule so it became more about learning what I needed to learn to be the leader I wanted to be.

You'd be surprised how much time you're on the phone and how much time you're watching TV. If you decrease your TV time and increase your reading time, magical things will start to change in your life.

Get yourself around as many high-level women as you possibly can. Seek them out, find them. Nobody will hold your hand, but if somebody reaches out to me, I will reach back out to them because it takes courage and they took that first step to do it.

Next, look and see what you're good at. If you don't know, then ask your friends to tell you five things you are good at. I guarantee you by the time you're done thinking and asking, you'll have identified ten strengths that will line up with what you love to do. Everybody has something that this world needs that they do really, really well.

You're here for a purpose, you have a gift, you need to share it with the world. And I don't think women are taught that enough. If you put in four to six hours a week, you'll start getting momentum and everything will shift for you. Everything.

Look at your expenses and see what you can cut out. The point is to find the money you can use to invest in you. Looking back, if I had paid $200,000 for that mentorship instead of $20,000, it would have been worth every dime because of the amount of money I have earned since then. I went from negative $50,000 to $1.2 million in 14 months. That's crazy. I had to learn skills and yes, I could have gone on YouTube and learned them myself, but I wanted to learn from somebody who was reputable and experienced.

When you find the right mentor and program, you are investing in them and in yourself. I always knew that I could depend on myself. I took a risk on myself. To me, it's no different from paying money to go to college and learn. You're learning a new skill. If you devote that time and effort into that new skill, you'll be able to do it.

Another thing to keep in mind is that you need to be coachable. My mentor had three rules: "Do what I say, when I say, no debate." She never said I couldn't ask questions, but I had to do what she said when she said with no debate. I think that's important because how many people do you know who would still try to debate with somebody who knows more than they do and makes more money than they do?

Don't listen to "broke" people. Do not listen to your family. Don't listen to your friends if they are not making more money than you. Unless they are in a place in their life where you also want to be, you have no business listening to them.

If you take the five people that you spend the most time with, add up their annual income and you divide it by five, that's the amount of money that you'll make, too. Get better friends to reach your big goals.

I have no problem charging $50,000 for somebody to spend three days with me. If you want me to teach you how to do what I do, you will invest what may feel like a lot. But I will make you money. You have to be coachable and willing to change your life.

I have a hard time with people who are okay throwing down hundreds of thousands of dollars on college knowing that most college graduates make $15 to $20 an hour. Those same people won't spend $20,000 on learning a new skill that will make them ten times that initial investment. And the truth of the matter is that 97% of people who pay all that money to learn never implement anything. And that's the saddest thing in the world to me. You must become a DOer!

If you want your kids to do something in their life, get up and do it yourself because they will watch you, see what you do, and follow in your footsteps. We want them to do all these things, learn all these things …..

Yet they're doing exactly what we do. Think about that.

We go to work, we come home, we make dinner, we watch TV, we go to bed. How much time do we really spend teaching our children things? Let's self-reflect as parents here and think about this. If you're working towards big goals, they will do the same. Bella sums it up this way, "If your kids have a Netflix binge issue, then so do you."

When I changed my mindset and my goals, I sat my kids

down and I said, "Look, you will have to help. If you step up, start carrying your weight and do more, my commitment to you is I will change your life!" To me that was a contractual agreement that I made with my children.

As parents, we have all these rules we want to lay down for our kids about all these things we don't want them to do, yet we're doing the exact same things. Kids don't listen to what we tell them; they see what we do. If we tell our children not to cuss, why are we doing it? I think parents forget that they set the example for their kids with their own behavior and actions.

The worst and best examples that our kids have is us. And regardless of what people think, our children love us.

I was able to come to terms with spending $20,000 on myself because I knew I was dependable, and I knew I wanted to show my kids by example that it's smart to invest in a mentor when you know you will also do the work.

You also have to understand that I have been through rejection and handled rejection my entire life. So I'm not scared of being told "NO" in a sales situation because I've already dealt with it and been through it.

Many people have gone through their entire life without being told "no." They've never been rejected for anything so the thought of that scares them to the point of paralysis. I tell people, "If you're a mother, an aunt, or a sister then at some point in time you've told your children, a sibling, or your niece or your nephew, 'No!'" The word or concept of "no" never slaps you in the face, it never bites you, it never physically hurts you. So why are you scared to hear the word? We have this unfathomable fear about rejection, but we must stop letting it stand in the way of our dreams.

Let me tell you about a woman who followed my program. Danielle is a realtor in Houston, Texas, but like so many realtors, she did not make a steady income. She was getting a divorce, and she needed extra cash flow, so she joined my Mobile Home Millions course. With two phone calls she was able to secure 15 mobile homes for free and made over $40,000 in three weeks. It's totally changed her life. And that's what I love doing: being able to see where people are, help them, and see how they completely turn their lives around.

Because so many people teach real estate and yet most people do not make the money they hope to do, I have developed things that set me apart in the industry. I teach people how to use apps on their phones to wholesale mobile homes virtually to make money.

For example, Mobile Home Millions did a live event on January 10th, 11th, and 12th, 2020. I took a big risk; I did a deal live during the event. The first night I took 45 minutes and got a home under contract. On the second day I had a buyer, and I sold it by the last day, Sunday. I literally plugged my phone in, and the audience saw the entire transaction all the way through to money in my bank account. To me, it's really how you value the people coming to you to learn.

For all of those people who have failed in real estate courses, you have to ask, are they really putting in the time they're saying they're putting in? Second, what's their motivation? Because if your "why" isn't big enough, then you will not do it. If you're not at a point where you're ready to change your life, you will not do it. You're just going to stay comfortable. There is a personal responsibility and accountability problem and it starts with mindset.

When I first started my journey, I had a ton of demons to face. One of those was being an enabler because I love people so much. I'm a giver and I give, give, give, and give to the point where I disabled them and enabled their bad behavior.

These are all those things you have to look at within yourself. If someone has taken a real estate course and they haven't made money, I encourage them to go back and read and listen to my suggestions, do the mindset work, model the behavior they want, and go do the work! For 30 days, devote time to your business every single day. And do not give up. Defaulting to a job should be your last resort, not your first.

Everybody thinks that working a 40-hour-week is the safest, most stable option to provide for yourself and your family. But the problem is, it's not like it was with our parents or grandparents when they got pensions.

Companies don't have pensions anymore. They MIGHT have 401(k)s. Well, guess what happens if the market crashes like it just did? Your 401(k) loses all its value. And what happens when the company goes out of business? All those matching dollars disappear.

In the first half of 2020, almost 40 million people lost those "stable" jobs. That's mind-boggling! Tens of millions of people were cut off from their ability to buy food, pay the mortgage, and get medicine, let alone indulge in fun. There are all these false beliefs about having a job. But my thing is that I'm a true believer in, "What you put out is what you get out."

For me, I'm not successful if my students aren't successful; my students' success is my success. If I do not have people who are using my formula and making money, it goes totally against the grain for me. I care about my students being able to do what they need to do.

I will tell you in my course, I offer three lifeline calls to my students. I have had over a thousand students and I've maybe had 20 of them use those calls. But all 20 who have used those calls have made money. I'm telling people all the time, please use your lifeline calls. That's what the team and I are here for.

I have regular live events, so if you think you'd like to attend one, contact support@mobilehomemillions.com and ask to be put on the waitlist.

In summary, there are a few things I really want you to know. One is, "It doesn't matter the cost of the shovel when you're digging for gold." It doesn't. And the other thing I want to say is that "the only claim that we, as women, have as to what our value and worth is comes through entrepreneurship."

That's it. That's the path to our claim. With entrepreneurship we get to set our own price on what we're worth and what our value is. You won't get that anywhere else. No corporate job will ask you, "What do you want to be paid? What do you think you're worth? What do you think is your value?"

But as an entrepreneur, I have a say in what I make, when I

get paid, and what happens to me and for me.

Working as an entrepreneur has helped me raise really good kids. Let me explain. I've fostered kids for eight years and I've raised over 60 children. I've put all my kids on a token system. Each child has five things that they have to do every morning after they get up: They have to make their bed, brush their teeth, comb their hair, get dressed, and pick up their area. And if they do those five things, then they get to put their five tokens in a jar—that's important.

Here's how our system works. Every day they start with five tokens and then we focus on one or two behaviors we want to change. Change only happens in children when you're focused and targeted, and it's been at least six months. (This can work for adults, too. Pick one or two habits you want to instill, focus only on them for six months, and create a carrot-and-stick accountability system for yourself!) The key to this is when you do this, everything else is out the window; you cannot rag on them about anything else. For example, we might focus on telling the truth and not having homework meltdowns. If they're doing homework and they have a meltdown, you say, "That's one. If you do it again, you will have to go take a token out of your jar."

I'm already training them to be personally responsible for their actions. They get one second chance to correct the behavior because we all make mistakes, but we have to learn from them. And when they make a mistake a second time, they take the token out because they are accountable for their actions and they need to implement the response.

It is not happening to them. I am not taking the token out for them while they passively receive that consequence. They do it. Because at the end of the week when they don't get their prize, then they are responsible for that because they took the token out. However, if they get defiant and Mom takes the tokens out, Mom takes all of them out.

Typically, after that, I never have to do anything again. At the end of the month, there is an extra reward for consistent, positive action-taking. They have a treasure box and they get to pick whatever they want to do for one day and each kid gets his or her own day to celebrate.

This is the way I've been able to instill good values into my kids in an entrepreneurial fashion. I also don't micromanage my kids for school. They know school is important. They know why it's important. You're responsible for your own poor grades.

I don't hover over my kids. I think that has helped me to nurture some amazing kids because I taught them how to self-manage and be responsible for their own actions. This led to Bella getting through her hardships and stepping voluntarily into my business in a big way, helping with my future and her own.

I want you to know what's possible. I was divorced with three children, in a new marriage, and unemployed. I went from that to receiving a ClickFunnels' Two Comma Club award because Bella and I had a sales funnel for Mobile Home Millions that made $1.2 million in 21 days! We broke a record. Then I generated $10.2 million in six months, breaking another record and earning the Two Comma Club X award.

And I recently learned that I have more awards and recognition than a few big name women business coaches. I say all this not to brag, but it's important for other women to see what they can accomplish when they focus and work. I changed my life and my family's life in a short period—less than five years! I could have had thousands of excuses for why my life would go nowhere and be nothing because of the trauma in my childhood. I was the "unwanted kid," the "throw-away girl," the girl that moved from home to home with all her belongings put in a trash bag (which happens every day in the CPS system,) but I have accepted none of that. I'm busy, I still do charity work, I have children; there's no excuse for anybody out there, ever. If I can do this...so can you! You can do this and live your best life. Love and Light!

Chimene

Bella Marsh

DOES EVERYTHING HAPPEN FOR A REASON?

Bella Marsh, Ecomm 4 Everyone
(www.ecomm4everyone.com)

"They may forget your name but they will never forget how you made them feel."

Maya Angelou

I always knew I was different. All the kids in school wanted to go to college, and I never saw college as an opportunity.

Since I was 11 years old, I wanted to go to Japan on a foreign exchange program in high school. I ended up going when I was 16 years old. It was a life-changing experience, and I was very blessed to have that opportunity. After returning, I did the rest of my school online. I graduated from high school in two-and-a-half years rather than the four traditional years. And that was all because I went to Japan. I took a lot of accelerated classes in high school to prepare for my trip to Japan.

One day I was sitting with my mom and she said, "Here is this guy named Russell Brunson." That was the day she introduced me to the ClickFunnels community. As I watched the video she had handed me, the things he said made sense. He talked about the 'perfect offer' and the 'red ocean' vs. the 'blue ocean.' That intrigued me. I had never done any sort of business in my life because I was only 17 years old.

We went to Funnel Hacking LIVE, and that was when everything really changed. My mom already had a business, and I'd been shadowing her for years. I've always shadowed my mom, learning from how she does things and how she handles certain situations. By watching her, I learned how to manage some pretty hard events in my life.

My journey with business started when I got a mentor. I had these false beliefs that I couldn't do anything online because I was only 17. I felt I was too young to understand how business worked. I hired a mentor, and she taught me a bit about Amazon. She wanted to test out a strategy with me. She taught me how to resell books to get the capital for my Amazon business.

Every weekend I would get a lot of books, because I had a lot of time, just not a lot of money. It was a superb business plan for me because I just drove and got books and then resold them. Then my mentor taught me how to shop smart.

She taught me this strategy on Amazon, which I used to teach, called retail arbitrage; you find products for a little cheaper—like on sale, not from China, or anything like that—but authentic products. And then you resell them on Amazon for the market price and keep the difference.

I realized that by doing this business, I can help people start an online business or entrepreneurship with minimal capital. I know there are a lot of drop-shipping methods. There's lots of private labeling from China, but it takes thousands of dollars to get started. I wanted to have a course for people who were like me, who didn't have a lot of money, didn't know where to start, and didn't have any direction. This would be something where they would be motivated as they watched the money come in.

My ex-boyfriend, Via, was my business partner; he quit his job and moved in with me. We wanted to launch online so we worked for nine months straight. The whole time we had motivation issues. We had a lot of problems and internal fears where we worried no one would buy and everyone would hate it.

Amazon is a hard market, but you have to learn which business works because there will always be customers no matter what kind of business you have. I tried to stay positive, telling him, "We got this. We got this." But once he started being unmotivated, I started getting unmotivated, too. I started sleeping on my couch and would sleep all day long. I was so unmotivated, and I felt like there was nothing left.

We were so close to launching. We had finished everything. I did most of the modules and the work and he just sat and watched videos on his computer. When we were about ready to launch our actual course, he came up to me and said, "I don't want to do this. I hate this. I hate working online. I hate everything. I hate entrepreneurship." When we went to Funnel Hacking Live the next year with my mom, he started doubting everything.

Some of his friends were famous YouTubers, and they told him, "Well, in those pyramid schemes, people can't get rich. It's a pyramid scheme because people can't get wealthy like that." I wondered if they were right.

Via ended up getting a normal job at a warehouse which was exhausting. He couldn't handle it. He went on a big trip with one of his famous YouTuber friends, and when he came back, I ended up finding out that he was being unfaithful to me. We had a big argument. I was crying; my self-esteem issues were terrible and that day, he took his life. I found him dead in our apartment with a gunshot to the head.

His friends, his family—everyone blamed me. They made a YouTube video about his passing. For me that messed me up. I felt so much blame and guilt that at one point, I wanted to die. I felt that it was my fault, and I wanted to join him. There were a lot of feelings about it.

I texted my mom when I found him. She came right away, and she was crying. The police were there, and she's screaming, "That's my daughter! Let me in. Let me go to my daughter." She took me to her home, and I stayed at her place for an entire month with my dog.

I didn't eat. I didn't drink. I just sat there and cried most of the time. My mom took me to Hawaii for a business trip—and of course, that's where I blossomed. She ended up taking me to swim with dolphins. I think that moment when I swam with dolphins and I got to see nature as what it was and how beautiful life is, I was incredibly thankful. And I think that's when I started trying to help myself and trying to help my healing.

Via's death has been the biggest hurdle in my life. For me, that's where everything fell apart and then fell back into place. My life has been crazy. But I've learned a lot, and I've definitely grown from it, and I think that's the best thing that could have happened.

I ended up meeting somebody who I wouldn't have met if life didn't take me down this path: my ex-boyfriend's co-worker's best friend. I ended up meeting him and I fell in love again. I told him about the business that I was doing and he encouraged me, "Why don't we launch it? Why don't we do it?" And I agreed, "You know what? Okay."

A week before Funnel Hacking Live, we busted out 18-hour days. We got it launched after Funnel Hacking Live. Within two weeks, I made $5,000 after months of making nothing. I was so happy. I could say to all the people who doubted us, "See, I knew this could work. I knew that this could work!"

With everything that has happened and seeing my mom go from 0-$10 million in a year and launching my own business from the ground up, I felt that my true calling was teaching people that are in the same position as me how to launch their expertise online on a budget. I will be targeting teens/young adults and I have so much joy when I think about the amount of people I can impact.

The biggest part of my journey was acknowledging that what happened to Via was not my fault. I tried everything in my power to stop what happened to him. I tried my best. I would often think, "If only things would have turned out differently." But then I look back, and I've met so many people because of what happened to me. I've gotten to inspire so many people. I spoke on stage at my mom's event in front of about a hundred people. It was my first ever motivational speaker session. Parents came up to me and cried asking me how they can have their child be like me. Everyone was very inspired by my speech and they all told me how much they loved it. It was an amazing feeling. I thought to myself, "For once I can help someone out. For once I can inspire someone who really needs to hear what I have to say." It made what I have gone through worth it.

Even though I'm not doing Amazon now, I have so many plans for the future. Especially with the new business I am launching. I want to be a motivational speaker because I want to help and inspire people. I don't plan on stopping there.

Hi, my name is Bella Marsh, and I'm the President and

CEO of Ecomm 4 Everyone.

My biggest goal right now with my business is that I want to help a lot of people enter entrepreneurship and make money online. I want to help them make money in a way that is not the "norm" and to have some kind of extra income, to impact the world.

One person I taught in the past was a mom. I thought it would be good for her because she could do it online and it doesn't take a lot of time; she would just need to dedicate maybe an hour or two in a day. If you already have your systems in place, it will only be about an hour a day. You just have to find the products you want to sell. I hope that my business will impact at least 500 people. That's where I see myself in three years - making a difference for 500 people.

I have had people come up to me and say, "You're so inspiring. You inspired me so much that I shared my story." I enjoy helping people share their stories. I would like to have a chance of being able to be an inspirational speaker because I know I will inspire so many people with the experiences I have been through.

I want to help my mom get the Two Comma Club C (for hitting $25 Million in revenue) award for her business. I love working with my mom. I get to help her by being all the backend support. I help her with the perfect webinar which is a system of how to use a webinar to generate sales. I also help her with all the support if things go wrong. I'm also the one who brings in the ideas and makes suggestions. She's 'the face,' and I'm behind the scenes.

Because we have so many students, we host our own live event. I also want to see more people walk across the stage at our live event because we have awards: We have a seven-figure, a six-figure, and a five-figure award in my mom's business. When I go to these live events, it's so amazing how many people are doing this and how many people want to meet my mom, Chimene. I want my mom to be known and famous in the mobile home real estate market. She is already, but I want people to recommend Chimene Van Gundy.

We're about to launch her podcast to bring more inspiration to people. We have a lot of stuff that will be happening. My mom has a future collaboration that I'm excited about for her. There will be so much stuff; she definitely keeps me busy! We are definitely the ultimate mother and daughter duo.

For others who want to go down this path, my first bit of advice is that even when you fail, you cannot just give up. The second thing is to follow someone you look up to, someone who's doing amazing things. For me, when we were working with Bryan Dulaney, I looked up to him. A lot of what he was doing were things that I've kind of implemented in my business just because I know what he's doing works.

Parents, this is for you. I want you to understand that your child is the one who is going to have to make the choice to become an entrepreneur. You can be their role model but it needs to be their decision. I know a lot of parents who try to force their lifestyle on their kids but in reality they are going to have to make that big commitment to want to become an entrepreneur on their own. By you being their role model it will change their mindset and future. That I can promise you just like it did with me.

Whether it's a mentor or someone who you look up to, I highly recommend finding someone who inspires you. Then see what they're doing and follow it—don't copy it, but follow it. I believe that is what Tony Robbins teaches people as well.

Another thing is that you will feel alone. I think that's what some people don't understand. When people think about entrepreneurship, they think about all these amazing things, but they don't see those times where you're behind the screen crying and feeling like a failure.

When my current partner quit his $22/hour job, we got a lot of hate from his family because it was a good-paying job. They would tell us, "You don't know this will work."

When it wasn't working, I felt defeated. It's a lonely process. Know that there are other people like you who are out there and it will be worth it. Do it now and you will be thankful later.

Have a routine, because if you don't have a routine, it's really hard to get to that level where you need to be. Because of what's going on now such as the Coronavirus, a lot of schedules have been messed up. Having a schedule helps you become more productive. You don't have to wake up at 2:00 AM or anything of the sort, but you just need to put yourself on a routine because it helps you get things in order.

Some people only work on their businesses four hours a day, before lunch, and they're done with their business. You don't need to spend 20 hours a day working on something that you are envisioning. You just need to do things step by step, because if you work so much, you'll get burned out.

Make sure you have those days where you just relax. That's something I wish I had learned sooner. That's how I got really burnt out at the beginning of working on my business for nine months. It took me nine months to build my business the first time and with my current partner, it took us two weeks. We barely used any of the previous material.

It's crazy to think I was so motivated that we could launch in two weeks versus my unmotivated self that took nine months, and in that time we were about to launch, but we didn't launch.

I do count that as a business failure because we were so close to launching. Instead, we thought, "You know what, let's listen to everyone else and let's be like the normal people. Let's get a normal job." And I actually remember putting in a resume, too. That was hard because I promised myself that I would never fill in a resume, but I put in a resume and started looking for jobs. Entrepreneurship isn't the norm.

But here are some things I've learned and some perspective I've gained about failure and learning lessons. When I was 12 years old, my mom and dad divorced, and I was very hateful towards my mom. I used to tell her very mean things, and I would make her cry and didn't realize it. My mom used to work three jobs and was a foster parent. I grew up with a bunch of foster kids and at any given time we'd have 10 or 12 kids in my home growing up. She's fostered 68 kids in total. Thinking back now as an adult, that's superhero work right there. I cannot believe that she did that. At the time I hated her. I hated that I moved schools and I just said so many mean things to her. I tried to make her and my stepdad divorce because I was super angry. I felt like my family was being torn apart.

Then one day my friend's mom died in a car accident. That opened my eyes because I realized that at any point in time, my mom could be gone. If someone who lost their mom had found out what I was saying to my mom, they would've given me the biggest ultimatum.

I still had my mom. I still had someone to guide me and someone who loved me unconditionally. My friend losing her mom put a bunch of love and gratefulness inside of me. I hadn't appreciated that my mom was working 10-hour days and three jobs until then.

Then there was my stepdad, who married my mom, a woman who had four kids. And my mom would say, "Who does that? Who marries a girl with four kids?" But he has been there for us, taught and treated us like his own kids, and he still does. I'm very grateful for the way things went looking back. Ultimately, I realize more and more that my step-dad is more of a dad to me then my biological dad.

My mom and I started rebuilding our relationship. I had

messed up a few times during my teenage years, and I was like, "Mom, please give me one more chance." And she gave it to me. I knew not to mess up because I couldn't go to Japan and something we agreed together was that my mom needed to trust me before I left for a different country.

The day that I came into this business was the day she started working with Bryan Dulaney and he asked me, "Hey, look, we need a videographer. We need all these people. Can you do this?"

And I said, "Yeah, I've been working on my videography stuff since I was 11, so let's go." I flew with her to San Diego, and they mapped out the perfect offer, and then I had to help her implement it. I helped her film the course for her online business teaching how to wholesale mobile homes.

I've done a lot of the backend stuff and throughout this process I have had a lot of parents ask me how they can get their kids to be like me, as I have mentioned earlier.

I respond with this answer on stage, too. I said, "You know, you want your kids to be successful like any other parent. But the thing is, we look up to you guys, as our parents, you know? Our parents are our heroes. If you want your kid to be success-ful, then you need to step up to be successful, too." The only reason I've ever done entrepreneurship is because my mom wanted to change her life and she took the initiative. She's very smart. She picks up on things; she knows how to differentiate herself in business. She's known in the real estate community, which is a male-dominated market. She's that smart.

A lot of parents will come up to me and say, "I wish my daughter and I could work together." I tell them, "Well, you become successful and they will follow in your footsteps. They really will." It's true because a lot of parents who are success-ful have successful kids. Their kids are doing amazing things. There's a pattern, and that is why what I am saying is true. Even when I grow up and have children, I want them to look at me and say, "I want to be like that."

Many people go to college and want to have that college experience. I already feel like I had that experience at such a young age. My mom trusted me so much that she let me go to Japan when I was 16 years old. My mom put her faith in me. For letting me go to Japan, my mom got so much hate. The people around her asked, "What kind of parent lets their 16-year-old daughter go to an unfamiliar country?" Mom would reply, "You know, we've mapped out what she had to do to go to Japan and then she did it." I went to Japan, and it changed my life. It was all thanks to my mom for letting me have this once-in-a-lifetime opportunity to go.

I came back and found I'd matured so much that I didn't understand a lot of what my former peers were doing. I was on another level and I even lost friends because of it. Then I got to meet Russell Brunson. I got to meet a lot of amazing people because of my mom. My mom always tells me, "Your network is your net worth."

I used to be very shy. I hated talking to people. I was very, very introverted. As I started learning, my mom would introduce me to all the people she knew. I was shy and wouldn't say anything. She ended up sitting down with me, and said, "You know, Bella, you will miss out on a lot of opportunities if you don't talk to people."

When I was at the Funnel Hacking Live 2020 event, I talked to a 14-year-old girl, Kathryn Woehlke, who had a podcast, and I was able to be a guest on her podcast. That was because I talked to her (and now we are in a book together!) The advice that I would give to anyone is to be open-minded and be extroverted.

Don't be afraid to start a conversation because you never know where your next million-dollar idea will come from.

When my mom went to this real estate event, she met the now-vice-president of her company. They're best friends to this day. She runs all the investment parts of my mom's business. If my mom didn't talk with her, this business would not even be here.

After I made $5,000 on the course I created, I thought about how it was an enormous milestone for me. With the help of my mom, she said, "Hey, this is what you're going to do with your business." I didn't do ads or anything. I just posted on my Facebook, asking, "Hey, is anyone interested in starting an Amazon business with minimal capital?" And I had 60 people respond. I took ten of those people at $497, then I accepted others for $997.

I spent hours privately teaching them my process. I've already made money off what I'm doing. I shared everything with them I did to make money.

I chose only ten because I wanted people who I thought would do well in this. I asked them, "Where do you see yourself? Where are you now? How much time do you have?" You don't need to have a lot of time, but you do need to dedicate at least eight or nine hours of your time in one-hour sessions. It could be every other day or once a week. I didn't want people to pay and then never do it. I wanted actual case studies. That's what people should strive for when first launching any kind of business.

A mom who is in Mobile Home Millions, Chimene's program, wanted me to do something with her daughter. I was all for it, saying, "Yes, let's do this." They trust me enough to let me teach them.

Another one of my students, Tyrone, was in Bible school to become a pastor, and he wanted some extra income to help people and to pay for his Bible school. And I was all for that. He's doing something that he's passionate about. It's hard to see when people aren't service-oriented, because once you think about how you can help your customers and how you can impact people, your life changes. Once you stop thinking about yourself, it changes the game.

The other two people I met from Funnel Hacking Live 2020 were 17- and 14-years old. I told them about what I was doing. After talking I realized that they were in the same position as me before.

They said, "We don't have a business, so this doesn't apply to us." You talk about business, and kids just kind of shut down because they're thinking, "This isn't for me. This isn't what I'm learning." But for them, they said, "Ooh, I'm interested. I do want to do something. I want to do something different."

That's how I chose the right clients for me. I taught another person, who was also in Mobile Home Millions, but he wanted to do something with his daughter. That's something that I was passionate about. I said, "Okay, if I'm able to help you guys, I will."

Some of my students inspire me because they want to do good things. They didn't say, "I just want money." They said, "I want to provide a little more for my family."

My biggest accomplishment in my own business is being able to teach my systems to a teen homeless shelter to help them grow their self worth and help them get started in entreprenuership. It is the best feeling in the world knowing I can help these teens see beyond their situation and focus on something that creates positive results.

Life is unexpected, and there are a lot of things that can happen. I feel as if I've been through a lot and I've learned a lot. When you're trying to succeed or do something, it feels as if life will always throw those hurdles at you, and you just have to figure out a way around them and overcome them.

Think about your future even when times are hard. What

is going to help you keep going is thinking about the amazing impact that you're going to make in people's lives. If you go to my website, https://www.ecomm4everyone.com/masterclass, you can get all the information on my program where I teach you how to launch your expertise online on a minimum budget.

All the best,

Bella

Kiana Danial

HOW CAN YOU MAKE YOUR MONEY WORK *FOR* YOU?

Kiana Danial is the CEO of Invest Diva.
(InvestDiva.com)

"Life begins at the end of your comfort zone."
Neale Donald Walsch

I was born and raised in Iran by a Jewish family during a Middle Eastern war—the Iran/Iraq war. Before the Iranian revolution, my dad was a very successful construction company CEO. He lost everything to the new Iranian regime. The government took over all of my dad's assets, closed his bank accounts, and were about to kill him. But he got lucky because the guy about to sign the execution order turned out to be his buddy from his military service days. Even though his life was spared, they still took all of his money and banned him from leaving the country.

So I grew up with very little.

When I turned 18, I ended up in Japan. I went to Japan on my own to study electrical engineering. I sucked at math, and I was the only girl in my class. All the classes were taught in Japanese. The reason I chose electrical engineering is that my dad was an engineer so I thought I should follow in his footsteps.

I was trying to prove myself. Electrical engineering did not work out for me, and I ended up learning Japanese which came in handy. My Japanese became so good that I ended up becoming a regular guest on a Japanese TV show where we debated social issues and all kinds of things—similar to The View in the U.S. I started making a bit of money, and I saved some of that money in the bank.

My money was just sitting in a Japanese bank and then bam, the 2008 market crash happened… the start of a recession. At the time, I knew nothing about finance. I heard the government was printing money to save the economy. What does that mean? Can they just print money out of thin air?

Apparently, they can. And that means that when you leave

your money in the bank, you're actually setting your money on fire. When the government prints money, that means that the supply of money is going higher in comparison to the demand, resulting in higher inflation. Higher inflation means that your future will be more expensive if your money is just sitting in the bank and not growing.

I thought to myself, this is not good. I should do something about this. The reason governments print more money is to encourage people to invest. Well, I don't know how to invest. So what could I do? I thought the logical thing to do is get a money manager to invest my money for me as an expert.

I found a financial manager, thinking he would do a better job than I would. But it turned out that's not true.

I learned that money managers invest your money in things that make them more money in commissions instead of what is best for you. I did some research, and I found out that certified money managers underperform the market average by 86%.

What is the market average? It's about 10% to 12% per year. They underperformed which meant that my money was barely growing. The final straw for me was that they had my money locked up in that fund. I didn't even have access to it. Years later, I got fired from my job and I needed money but I couldn't access it without paying a massive penalty.

Why would I give my money to somebody who barely grows it? They're taking commissions out of it and locking my money up, and if I want to get my money back I have to pay a penalty. All of this made no sense to me. So, I took things into my own hands and I became obsessed about learning about finance and investing.

I started working on Wall Street. I enrolled in the certified financial planner (CFP) program and certified market technician (CMT) program among other personal finance and investing related educational courses. That's when I realized that personal finance is not as hard as everyone makes it sound. It all sounds very complicated because if it sounded easy, people wouldn't go to the money managers and certified financial planners.

While I was learning all this stuff I wondered why I was always the only girl, whether it was in an engineering class or on Wall Street. I saw research that showed that women are actually better at investing than men because of their natural instincts; however, for many women it's intimidating just to get started.

I had two choices: I could either become and act as a

certified financial planner and make money that way or create a new thing and empower people to invest on their own. I chose the second path, and that's where I am today.

At the start, it was frustrating. I really wanted to help moms, and I kept getting male students. I had money coming in and it was great. There were people who were searching for my books, reading my books, taking my course, and making money. But every once in a while, I would just get very frustrated at the gender imbalance.

The brand name of my business is Invest Diva. I have my toddler in the background when I create my YouTube videos. I literally say, "Hey, Invest Diva is about women's empowerment." But I would still get guys. I wondered, "Why aren't women really getting into this?"

Then, for better or for worse, here comes COVID-19. I started during a recession and I'm still making money as the market goes up and down. I feel like my story finally started resonating with moms and women and them wanting to make this happen for their children. Before, when things were good, everybody was making money and people were not looking at financial management.

When everything hits the fan, that's when people get

paranoid and start taking action. That's exactly what happened and we're seeing a lot of moms now. The community has grown by 100%.

This recession will create a lot of opportunities for people. Actually, recessions make the most millionaires because the ones prepared for it are the ones who get in at the lowest point and make a ton of money.

Recessions are actually great opportunities. If you can't invest during this recession, you want to prepare so that you can invest in the next recession. I feel like people are now seeing it. It's a movement now and I'm very, very proud of it.

I'm an entrepreneur first and an investor second, and I teach my entrepreneurs about investing. Sometimes people wonder if I'm making so much money investing, then why am I teaching? I made cash by being an entrepreneur. You can rarely become a millionaire just by investing and starting with, let's say, $500. You would have to be super lucky, and I don't want luck to be part of my investment strategy. The circle of my wealth is like this: I make money from multiple revenue streams, Invest Diva being one of them. Then I make my money work for me by investing. Then I invest in myself, I add onto my revenue stream, and then I invest the rest of it again.

So that is the cycle: Invest in yourself, make cash, then make that cash work for you. That is the only way to true wealth because if you're just making money and you're not putting your money to work for you, you may even be broke.

We know so many entrepreneurs who are making millions of dollars, but they're broke because they are not financially literate. Why do you think 90% of lottery winners lose their money? That's because financial literacy is not a side effect of wealth. Wealth is a side effect of financial literacy. They go hand in hand. What you need to have before you invest is an understanding of your risk tolerance, an understanding of your financial situation, and an understanding of your financial goals. Based on these three things, you can create an investment strategy.

This does not mean that you need to have a ton of money to invest. Many people think they should wait to invest until they have $15,000 to invest. That's a myth. When I started investing in myself and learned about how to create investment strategies, I started out with only $500. I turned that $500 into $53,000 within three years because my approach was longer-term and strategic.

I knew where I wanted to go, I knew my risk tolerance, and

I was investing not based on market noise, but based on what I call the Invest Diva Diamond Analysis. It analyzes the markets from five different points. It's called IDDA for short.

What's even more interesting is that the $53,000 eventually helped us with the down payment on the house we live in now. My husband and I had found a house that was exceptional, but we were $50,000 short. And I was like, "Oh my God, let me look at my account." His family lived in Australia and I'm from Iran. We wanted our families to visit us, especially since we were growing our family. We needed a bigger house so that $53,000 came in handy.

The lessons? First, trial and error will probably be very costly to you. Second, you don't need a ton of money to get started. The sooner you get started, the better. And third, don't try to time the market because the market noise is only there for clickbait.

That is the media's job. Don't fall for the hype and the format of the media. Have a strategy and stick to it. Then your investments and your life will become a lot easier.

Hi, my name is Kiana Danial, and I'm the CEO of Invest-Diva.com.

My PowerCourse is eight weeks and you have lifetime

access to it. It takes you through how to measure exactly where you stand financially, how to set up your financial plan to retire wealthy, how to navigate through the financial markets, how to set up your investment system like a pro, and how to create perfect investment strategies for your unique risk tolerance and financial goals.

In Week 6, we learn how to select the perfect investment in different market conditions. Week 7 talks about exactly how much to invest, when to buy, and when to take a profit. And finally, Week 8 is how to beat the boys of Wall Street at their own game.

So that's the PowerCourse, and it's eight weeks and it's super awesome, but you can always go back to it because your financial situation changes over time.

Time in the market beats timing the market. The more time you have to invest, the better. We've heard stories of cab drivers who started investing early and finished with millions of dollars in their bank accounts. The sooner you get started for you and for your children, the better. Should I start investing right now? Yes, because you can always tell when the recession is about to hit; we get the indicators, so you just get out. I started one of my investment accounts in 2019 when I knew a market crash was coming.

I just set my profit targets a little earlier, and I got out in February. We made money. There's always opportunity in the markets. There is nothing worse than getting affected or influenced by fear of missing out or the hype that you have to get the first foundations right before jumping in and just buying some stock that somebody told you about.

To me, that is the biggest mistake that investors can make. The sooner you get started with education, the better you can identify investment opportunities no matter what part of the business cycle and the economic cycle we are in. For your children this will get them started on the right foot.

One myth I want to dispel is that investing requires a ton of time. Moms are busy. The first thing that comes to their mind when they think about investing is that, "Oh my God, I have to be stuck watching my screen all day." That is absolutely not true.

I only spend an hour on Tuesdays to manage the four portfolios I'm in charge of. This includes mine, my husband's, my dad's, and my sister's portfolios. Combined, these have over a hundred assets.

That is the same time I go live for my members. We call them the Premium Investing Group (PIG) members. Every Tuesday morning at 10:00 AM I go live for only one hour because you can instruct your broker to buy and sell certain investments.

For example, let's say I want to buy Apple stock when the price reaches $400 because of the analysis that I've done based on my course. I will not try to time the market by sitting with my eyes glued to my screen all day waiting to see if it will hit $400.

Instead, my broker will track it for me. The stock may reach my target price in two weeks, in two months, or even a year from now. The point is my order is still sitting there, so I can just go about my day. The same thing happens when taking a profit, which means selling. Let's say I bought one share of Apple stock at $400 and now you want to take profit at $500 Again, you tell your broker, and whenever the stock hits that price, sell it.

Calculating those numbers is what I teach in my "Make Your Money Work For You PowerCourse." It is a combination of analyzing the markets from five different points. The first three points are about the market or the asset that you're trying to invest in.

Number one is the fundamentals. What do the fundamentals cover? Here, you're answering questions like: How well do you know the asset? How is the asset doing? What's the company about? What do you expect them to do in the future?

Step number two is understanding the asset's price action. For that I have this little trick that I found, thanks to having lived in Japan and speaking Japanese. There was this Japanese indicator that I've written a book about, called ICHIMOKU. I put it on the charts and it just gives me the indicators. No math needed at all. I set that price and it has three levels.

Step number three is market sentiment, which is what other investors and traders are doing. I normally go against them, because every time the markets are up and the media is saying to buy, that is when the price is really, really high. It's like buying bathing suits at the beginning of the summer when everyone is talking about going to the beach. Whereas, if you wait for the off-season, everything will be on sale. Personally, with shopping, I shop for bathing suits at the end of summer and I shop for ski gear at the beginning of summer. The same thing applies to investing. Market sentiment analysis is like waiting for the Black Friday of the stock market when everything goes on sale.

Step number four is getting the first three points to match your risk tolerance. Your risk tolerance is going to be low, medium, or high. Risk tolerance has two components: 1) your ability to take a risk (How much money do you have? What is your age? Are you a parent? How old are your children?) and 2) your willingness to take a risk. There is a reason women are better investors. They naturally don't want to take higher risks and that comes in handy. Your risk tolerance gives you an answer as to what to invest, when to invest, and how long you can wait.

Step number five brings all four steps together, resulting in a strategy. These five steps are what I teach in my "Make Your Money Work For You PowerCourse."

With education, it's important to have financial literacy and to understand your financial situation. All you need is a fourth-grade-level education. That's why a lot of the moms in my group study my course with their children because I encourage the moms and the dads in our group to talk about money with their families. Money and sex are the two things that contribute to the highest amount of divorces. So once you get on the same page about money, your marriage will get better. Therefore, I encourage my members to talk about money with their spouses.

To be honest with you, I had the same problem with my husband. My husband and I are very, very different when it comes to managing money. I am the saver, and he is the spender. His motto for life is that you never know when you're going to die; You might as well just use your money.

He gets this because his dad passed away right as he was planning to retire and enjoy life. His mom and dad didn't get to use the money they were saving for retirement. As for me, I saw my dad lose everything, so I just want to hang onto every penny I have. When we first got married, it frustrated me.

We had to go to therapy and talk about it openly so that we could get on the same page. I encourage people to take my course with their partners. Women must learn how to manage their finances because women live longer than men.

One of the biggest myths is that the husband will always take care of the finances. The average age of widowhood is only 59, and not even the millionaires are immune to that. In fact, they may be even at a higher risk. Kobe Bryant died recently, and I don't know how much his wife was prepared for that. Imagine losing a husband and a daughter at the same time.

Do you know if your financial advisors have your best interests at heart? There is a very high chance those financial advisors will take advantage of the situation when the person is grieving. I want to emphasize this point. Lady Gaga, a nine-time Grammy award winner, went bankrupt and was $3 million in debt after her Monster Ball tour. Why? Because she wasn't investing; she was letting her financial advisors handle everything. I want to stress that even if you are making money, that is not going to make you wealthy.

My daughter is two years old, so I'm not talking about money to her yet, but I'm planning to introduce her to the concept of spending money on investments. I only shop for things that add value to my life and are considered an investment. I have my own business, which is great, so I only buy things I know will make a return on the investment.

That is the number one rule of financial literacy.

I was fortunate because as a kid, seeing my parents struggle with every penny and not having enough money every day, they had to make hard decisions. We didn't live in the U.S., so we didn't have credit cards.

The unfortunate thing about the U.S. is that you can just buy whatever you want on a credit card and get into an immense amount of credit card debt. That was mind-blowing to me. People were buying things with money they didn't have.

When I was seven, I learned that you don't buy things if you don't have the money. You really have to teach your children. I think corporations developed credit cards to make them money. You do not understand how much money these corporations and the banks make by charging you interest and fees on credit cards.

That's the reason they don't teach you financial literacy in middle and high school. If they did, the corporations wouldn't make as much money.

Money has become political. No matter which political party you support, it's in their best interest to make sure you are not financially literate. My nephew is nine years old, and he understands how to buy things. The sooner you talk about money with your kids and teach them not to spend money they don't have, the better, because you want this habit to develop early on.

There is this amazing analysis that my coach David "Kombucha" Lindenbaum talked about, which is the Marshmallow Theory. They researched 40 children and said, "We're going to give you one marshmallow and we're going to leave the room. If you eat that marshmallow right now, you're not going to get a second one. If you wait for us to come back into the room and then eat it, you're going to get two marshmallows." They did this over and over again. They followed those children for 40 years, and they found the children who did not eat the first marshmallow and waited for the second one overwhelmingly succeeded in life.

It's called delayed gratification. It's not just about money. If you delay gratification to watch TV, then you can go and read a book and learn something and add to your skills. If you delay the gratification of eating ice cream, then you're going to get healthier. If you're the kind of mom who is passionate about health and being healthy, eating veggies, and working out, then money is right up there. The minute you start talking about healthier children is the moment that you need to start talking about money to your children.

The most heartwarming story I have about someone who has worked with me is about Misty. Misty is a yoga instructor and she's raising children while working. She has two teenage children, and she didn't have a ton of time to spend in front of her computer. She's also been battling Lyme disease for many years. Her illness isn't covered by insurance.

After her mom passed away and left her with an inheritance, she wanted to do something with it. She knew she wanted to invest it but didn't know how to do it. The first thing she did was search for information about investing and she heard from her brother about this company that was going to be the next big thing. She put all of her inheritance into that company.

That company went bankrupt, and she lost all $100,000 of her inheritance. That is when she came to me for help. When I got her into our program, she didn't have that lump sum of money. She had to pay for her healthcare out of pocket. She wasn't making much, and she was getting into a huge amount of debt. She got into the system, putting in the work for eight weeks, and she spent some time figuring things out.

When she was done, she could pay off her medical expenses. She was able to make $16,000 and put that towards her medical expenses for that quarter. Now she makes even more money than that.

Misty is one of many, many students and success stories that we've had. We have so many single moms who get into our program. Single moms have to be in charge of their finances.

I just got a testimonial from one of my students in Italy who is a single mom. Investing intimidated her. She thought it was hard and akin to gambling. Then she got into the program and now she's rocking it. She's a translator in Italy and taking care of her daughter by analyzing the markets and investing on her own. She's kicking ass which is pretty cool.

You can invest from any part of the world. That's the beauty of the current situation. The Internet has brought everyone together, and no matter where you are in the world, you can invest in the U.S. stock market. You can invest in the markets of your local country. You can absolutely invest from anywhere in the world as long as you have an Internet connection.

Your investment timeline is the most important thing. That's why investment strategies should be different. I finally started investing for my dad a few years ago and he's 80. Obviously, his investment portfolio is different from my investment portfolio. I'm a mom, I have a husband, we both have jobs and we have a toddler, and we're thinking about growing our family.

My dad, who is already retired, doesn't have 30 years to wait on a stock market rebound. That is one of the main things you have to consider when you're developing your investment strategy. With my dad, I invest for him in dividend-paying stocks that pay an income no matter what the market cycle is.

Why wouldn't everyone invest in dividend stocks? Well, for me, it doesn't make sense. I earn my income from my business and I'd rather bet on investments that have a huge growth potential over three to five years because that's the timeline I'm looking at. I'm looking to invest so I can put away money for my daughter's college expenses. I'm looking to invest so I can leave money for my daughter and potentially buy a second house or a vacation home. I have a longer investment timeline.

These things are some of the things I teach in my eight-week course. The first four weeks are just about the foundation because when you get the foundation right, the rest is super easy. You just pick the stocks suitable to that and then I teach you exactly how to find them, and that's it. The timeline is directly influenced by your age, your family situation, your financial situation, and your financial goals.

The first step for people is to just attend my on-demand Masterclass, which runs every day (https://learn.investdiva. com/yes). I go through everything and then I lead them to becoming a Premium Investing Group member.

When it comes to buying and selling, you have to put your emotions aside. Some people get super excited whenever they are right about an investment choice because they are in it for the challenge. On the flip side, whenever there is a loss, and I've seen it in my other students as well, they get very emotional and think they have to go make up for that loss.

Remember... The markets are not about math, they're about psychology. I just want to leave you with that because women are naturally better with emotional intelligence. That's why they are actually better at investing.

Kiana

Leanne Woehlke

CAN YOU FIND THE GIFT IN EVERY SITUATION?

Leanne Woehlke is a Certified Life Coach, and a 1,200-hour yoga teacher. She is the Chief of Possibility at Epic Yoga. (epiyogacenter.com, epicyogaonline.com and TeachYogaOnline.com)

"When you are inspired by some great purpose, some extraordinary project, all of your thoughts break their bonds. Your mind transcends limitations; your consciousness expands in every direction; and you find yourself in a new, great and wonderful world. Dormant forces, faculties and talents become alive and you discover yourself to be a greater person than you ever dreamed yourself to be."

Patañjali

Each life is a gift. The question is, can we appreciate that in the moment?

Many people take for granted those seemingly non-eventful days until they are gone. Growing up I was the scrappy kid with big ideas and even bigger dreams. My entrepreneurial ventures included backyard carnivals, lemonade stands, newspaper routes, and even selling popsicle stick houses, which I was sure were worth several thousand dollars. While none of my childhood ideas were as lucrative as I might have liked, the lessons were invaluable and helped me develop the mindset and tenacity I have today.

Yogis believe that each of us are born with a specific number of breaths. When we exhaust that number, our days are done. I'm not sure I entirely agree with that, but I do believe that many people live their life as if they have an unlimited amount of time. I learned this lesson the hard way. My Dad died unexpectedly in a car accident when I was 18 years old. I found myself at a crossroads. I could either feel sorry for myself for losing my Dad so young, or I could create a bigger purpose and make my life matter.

Losing my Dad made me realize life was fragile. There was no guarantee of a long life. This lit a fire under me to make my time here on the planet matter. I wanted to make a difference for others. I just wasn't sure what that was yet.

I went on to get a Master's Degree in Experimental Psychology, with the intention to go on and get a PhD. However, upon graduating I was shocked at the miserable job prospects. I was making more money selling cosmetics at Nordstrom than the starting salaries in my field. I began to wonder if I had wasted six years and thousands of dollars on education. This just didn't make sense. I thought that if I got an advanced degree, I'd get a corresponding salary. I was wrong.

Regardless, I made the leap to the corporate world and began to work my way up the ladder. I was monitoring clinical drug trials, traveling 75% up to 100% of the time. I was making what most people would consider "good" money but felt nauseous every day on my way to work. Literally, the stress was to a point that I felt physically ill at the idea of going to the office. The constant travel and intense timelines were clearly taking a toll.

The researcher in me began to notice that on the days I did yoga before going to work I didn't feel like I was going to vomit. It appeared that yoga was in some way modulating the stress. I didn't know how, but I knew from my background in science that something was going on.

My body was screaming at me on a daily basis. I came to the realization that life was about more than money. It didn't matter what was in my bank account if I felt sick every day going to work. This high-stress lifestyle was not sustainable long term. I asked my employer for a leave of absence, which they denied, so I did what any "responsible" 28-year-old would do; I quit my job, put all of my belongings in storage, and left to go to India to study yoga.

When I arrived in India it became clear that I didn't need to go halfway around the world to find the answers I was searching for; I just needed to get quiet enough to listen to that still small voice within. The problem was it was being drowned out in the noise of everyday life. While in India, I remember telling another yoga student that I wanted to do something that "mattered" and that felt more in line with my purpose. She told me not to underestimate the contribution I was making. To trust the journey. Little did I know, she was spot on!

After returning from India, I went back to the corporate world, but this time I was committed to bringing more balance. I began teaching yoga part time at my office, in hopes of sharing a practice that may help others navigate the stress of a modern world. One day a woman who worked for me and regularly attended my yoga class came into my office. She asked if she could shut the door and talk to me. I said, "Of course." I thought she was going to hand in her resignation. Instead, she sat down in the chair next to my desk and said, "I've suffered with depression my entire life. Yet I've noticed that since we started doing yoga, I don't feel as bad." This is a theme I would continue to hear over and over throughout the next 20 years.

The summer after I returned from India, I met my husband and we got married three years later. I was pregnant within six months and we were elated. However our initial excitement morphed into fear when our 20-week ultrasound revealed that our son had a rare genetic anomaly which doctors deemed, "incompatible with life." The doctors had suggested I terminate the pregnancy, sort of a "sanitizing" of the situation in an attempt to avoid the inevitable. It was as if they were saying if I was no longer pregnant, the pain would just magically vanish. I had to convince them that I understood the odds, that I knew if our son did make it to term, it was likely his life would be short and that he would have developmental delays. I didn't think this one was for me to decide. I wanted to leave this one in God's hands and hold space for a miracle. I believe that each life is a gift, no matter how short, no matter how brief, and so I decided to roll the dice and give this little guy a chance.

Our son was stillborn at 32 weeks. His passing was devastating, but there were also miracles… feeling him do flips in my belly when I ate jelly beans, seeing his sweet face, his downy black hair, and his resemblance to my husband. His brief life taught me the gift of radical acceptance. I was able to learn to accept things exactly as they are, exactly as they are not. From that vantage point I was able to embrace circumstances I never would have chosen and make the best of it. From acceptance, comes choice. And I chose to view his life as a gift, even if losing him left a huge hole in my heart.

As I tried to make sense of his loss, I learned you can't circumnavigate pain. The only way out is through. I knew I had to sit with the grief, to acknowledge it, feel it, and then move it out of my body. Yoga helped. Grief, or any other emotion, can get "stuck" in the body. Or as somatic psychology explains, "The issues are in the tissues." From my years of grad school I understood the mind-body connection and knew the grief needed to move out of my body, just as when my Dad died, although now I had more tools.

I believe that any experience we have in this life is so that we can share it with another. Any experience, even the most painful or difficult, can be used for good by helping another navigate a similar situation. I would have this belief put to test when I opened my yoga studio.

Almost a year later I found out I was pregnant again. Again we were told there were issues. And again I chose faith. To sit with what is, and hold space for the miracle. When our daughter, Kathryn, was born, the cord was wrapped around her neck, which provided quite a dramatic entrance into this world. Soon after her birth, a team of doctors were ushered into the room. "What are we looking for?" they asked. I sighed in relief when they reported, "Everything looks good." I took that as a sign that the issues we were worried about prenatally were no longer present.

The first few weeks of Kathryn's life were filled with lots of doctor appointments and therapists. I was going to give this baby any, and every, tool or resource that might help her thrive. At some point, I decided to stop looking for something to be wrong and decided to just love her. I figured we could deal with any issues, if and when they showed up. Worrying about what "could be" wrong was not going to serve any of us.

Kathryn arrived in this world just in time. Little did we know what the coming year had in store, but she would serve as my "true north," or point of focus, during that period. Having a young child forced me to stay focused on the present moment. In yoga, we call that one-pointed focus "drishti."

Exactly four months after Kathryn was born, and eleven days after I quit my corporate job, my husband, John, was diagnosed with a rare and aggressive form of cancer. From my work in pharmaceuticals I knew how to research protocols and wasn't afraid to ask questions. Ah, now I understood what the woman in India was saying about not undervaluing my path. My experience in research and drug development would prove invaluable over the next year as John went through chemo, then high-dose chemo and two stem cell transplants.

Life again seemed to show me that no matter how much money you have, it's not enough if you didn't have your health. As Gandhi said, "It is health that is real wealth." Yoga provided the stress relief in another seemingly unimaginable time. Breathing through the emotion and taking things one breath at a time got me through the unthinkable… all the while toting Kathryn along to every one of John's treatment and doctor appointments.

When the cancer returned after John's first four rounds of

chemo, I decided we would supplement his conventional treatments with a slew of alternative therapies. I believe that the body has an innate desire to keep itself healthy. The body tries to maintain homeostasis. It's when things get out of whack that cancer, or other dis-ease, manifests in the body.

Thankfully one year later, John was cured and life went back to "normal." It felt like we were given a second lease on life. Once again, we were reminded of the importance of health, not "abs of steel", but holistic health which I define as being able to have the strength, energy and stamina to do the things you want and go to the places you choose.

Life seemed to settle into a comfortable rhythm. John took a new position, Kathryn began pre-school, and I began various projects. We decided it was time to expand our family, however due to all of the chemo John received, we were forced to turn to IVF.

As we began our third IVF attempt, I celebrated my 40th birthday. Since I was 40, I had to go in for my first mammogram. When the tech left the room and came back with a doctor I knew things were not "normal." The doctor explained that they had found "cysts." Then he said, "We have to do a biopsy." My mind was reeling. At the time I was pumped full of hormones for IVF. I knew if it was cancer, the additional hormones would cause it to spread faster. Thankfully the biopsy showed the cysts were non-cancerous and we resumed the IVF cycle. However, at my next appointment with the fertility doctor, we learned the conditions were not right for an embryo transfer and the cycle would yet again be cancelled. After the biopsy scare, I realized in my quest to have another baby, there was a possibility I could end up leaving my daughter motherless. At that moment, I knew I was done with IVF. There would be no more cycles, no more drugs, no more attempts. I trusted God had other plans for me.

I called John from the parking lot and told him the news. "The cycle was cancelled, I'm done with IVF, and I am going to open a yoga studio." He tried to reassure me that we could try again, that there were other options. He said, "We can talk when I get home." I said, "No, I'm done. There's nothing to talk about."

Tony Robbins says, "In moments of decision, your destiny is shaped." In that moment, I knew my decision would change not only my own life, but the lives of many others. I had to let go of the life I planned and instead accept the opportunity that was actually in front of me. I gave up the idea of being a "family of four" and instead fully embraced my little trio. My small but mighty family would give me the bandwidth and agility to create my EPIC dream.

EPIC is defined as "an episode in the life of a woman/man in which heroic deeds are performed or attempted... of massive proportion." As I searched for a name for my studio, EPIC jumped out at me. It seemed to sum up my journey and what I hoped others would find through these practices. I wanted to share the principles that had allowed me to get through some of the most difficult times in my life and reframe them powerfully. I wanted to help people realize the potential inside of themselves, and to rewrite their narrative through an empowered, inspired lens. I was compelled to help people shift their mindset and to be able to differentiate sensation from pain. I wanted to help people remember how to dream again. To reconnect with that which inspires, and call forth the best version of themselves. The one that they may not have even known existed. I wanted to invite them to discover their own EPIC journey.

Through the practice of breath and movement, layers of stress drop away and habitual patterns of tension begin to dissolve. The nervous system is balanced and pure potentiality opens up. I knew that others in my community needed this message. I felt opening this studio was my calling.

The day the money transferred into my account for the business, I got a call from the leasing agent saying they were not going to lease to us due to concerns about parking. Fearing my studio dream was slipping away, I took an hour and went to a yoga class. When I got back, John sat me down and told me we needed to talk. That is never a good thing. He told me the doctor called, and said they "saw something" on the PET scan. He was about five years post-treatment, which is usually the point they tell you don't have to worry about it any more. The doctor told him they needed to do a biopsy and that it was "in the lung." Again, not a good thing. Due to the amount of chemo John had previously, we knew if this was cancer, his treatment options would be limited. I began to feel my dream of opening a studio slipping away, as I geared up for another fight against cancer.

That night we went to dinner in San Francisco with my brother-in-law. As we made our way into the city, and round a turn, we came face to face with a neon sign that said "EPIC." And right then, I knew that regardless of the biopsy results, I needed to go forward with the studio.

Thankfully the biopsy was inconclusive. Although the surgeon told me it was "cancer" on the day of the procedure, the results from the lab were not clear. They chalked it up to some sort of odd "fungus" in Tennessee. We'd take it as long as it wasn't cancer. They gave John some sort of antifungal prescription for a while and it seemed to resolve. Again I was reminded of the importance of just sitting with things and not jumping to conclusions. This seemed to be a recurring theme in my life!

We opened EPIC when Kathryn was starting kindergarten. Initially it was a fun little hobby project for me. One night during dinner at a restaurant with white butcher paper and crayons on the tables, I mapped out the EPIC revenue model. I explained to John, my finance executive husband, he was paid in dollars, and I drew a bunch of dollar signs. Then I explained that I was paid in "joy" and I made lots of little happy faces. I explained the problem was that we were paid in different currencies. Sort of like dollars versus Monopoly money. We both knew this was code for, "I'm not making any money but I'm having a lot of fun."

Eventually I realized being "paid in joy" does not pay the bills. In business you trade your life force, your time, and your energy for some sort of pay off. I would regularly hear stories from clients of how, "EPIC changed my life" but the reality was, the financial well-being of my family was not being positively impacted by my business. Over the years I've found that many heart-based entrepreneurs just want to give it all away, which is great, but not if they can't pay their bills. There is nothing enlightened about being broke.

With this realization, I began paying myself and looking at EPIC as a business, not a community service project, although we continued to serve our community at a very high level. I realized my desire to not pay myself and to "give it all away" was not sustainable and if things kept going that way, I would be burnt out and my business would not be viable for the long haul. It is the responsibility of a business owner to be profitable, to ensure that business is able to survive, and serve the community for many years.

Hi, my name is Leanne Woehlke, and I'm the Chief of Possibility at EpicYoga. (epicyogacenter.com and epicyogaonline.com) In the corporate world, I was working under tight timelines with huge dollars at stake. I realized there was more to living a successful life than dollars in a bank account, with no time to enjoy the fruits of your labor. I hung up my corporate suit and traded it in for yoga pants. I began teaching the tools of transformation and mindfulness to people who felt disconnected and unfulfilled with their 9-5 job.

At EPIC, we help people reconnect with their breath, body and the deeper meaning of their lives. The practice helps shed layers of tension and stress, leaving clients feeling more connected with their life force. In yoga, we call that "prana." This practice is needed now more than ever, with depression and anxiety at an all-time high, with one in every ten Americans, and 23% of women in their 40's and 50's, taking antidepressants. Pharmaceutical companies often "massage" the data to eliminate less desirable adverse events and improve the risk-benefit profile. Having witnessed that first hand, I felt even more passionate about providing viable options to people that did not require them to take a drug for the rest of their life.

The yogis have known about the power of the breath and yoga practices for thousands of years. Modern science is just now beginning to catch up and validate the effect on self regulation and vagal nerve tone. Yoga has been shown to help with hypertension, diabetes, stroke, depression, anxiety, and many other conditions. It's been said, "If yoga was a pill, everyone would be taking it."

In yoga we talk about removing all that is not true. The false beliefs, the limiting thoughts, the things that keep people stuck and unfulfilled. Sort of like a sculptor strips away the excess marble to reveal the masterpiece. Research studies have shown yoga reduced identification with and attachment to the ego. As one strips away negative self talk and upgrades the narrative identity, health improves. "Tell a better story, enjoy better health."

In the EPIC Teacher Training program, we utilize modern coaching principles coupled with ancient yoga practices to help an individual live their best life. We strip away the not-true narrative to allow one to connect to a deeper calling. This program has been nicknamed "Soul Camp" and has gone on to produce many entrepreneurs living their dreams, making a difference in the lives of their clients, and actually generating income!

Two years ago I went to Funnel Hacking Live in Nashville. I had never heard of Russell Brunson or Click Funnels, but a friend mentioned they had gone the year prior and that, "If you get one idea you can implement, it will be worth it." I bought a ticket and sat in the audience in amazement. Russell was talking about things that were never discussed in the heart-based entrepreneurial world. It felt like this was the knowledge I needed to move my business forward. I knew sharing this information would also help others be able to re-think their businesses in ways that would allow for long term success. As I sat there I kept thinking, "I wish I could share this with Kathryn…. This information would be so powerful for kids." When Russell shared that his elite coaching program included a "family friendly" event, I was sold.

I joined Russell's Two Comma Club Coaching program and began learning and implementing as fast as I could. It felt like new life was being breathed into my business. I knew the yoga principles and practices worked, and now I had the strategy and techniques to take my business to the next level.

For me, it was important that my daughter see me succeed. She had been a huge part of EPIC since the beginning, from picking out logos, ordering and organizing retail, discussing marketing messages, and greeting clients at the front desk. I think it's important for kids to be able to see non-traditional jobs that allow more freedom than the standard 9-5.

In August of 2019, we attended Unlock The Secrets, the event Russell created for families. Initially my husband and daughter were planning on sightseeing during the day.

However, after meeting Jamie Atkinson and learning about podcasting, Kathryn decided she wanted to learn more. She sat through every session, taking copious notes and soaking in every word. One of the days I had an early morning podcast with a former pro baseball player turned yogi. I woke up at the crack of dawn to head to the meeting. Kathryn woke up, realized I had already left and made my husband, John, get up to take her down to meet me. She actively participated and asked relevant questions. I was so impressed with how she conducted herself and the quality of her questions and ability to interview a complete stranger. During Unlock The Secrets she mustered up the courage to ask questions in front of the crowd and meet other young entrepreneurs at lunch. Seeing my daughter develop even more confidence was worth every penny of the program.

Five years ago I began working on an online Yoga Teacher Training School www.teachyogaonline.com. After Unlock The Secrets I began consolidating my content and finalizing the program. Little did I know I would be moving my entire business online in just a few short months. In The Obstacle is the Way, Ryan Holiday states, "A business must take the operating constraints of the world around it as a given and work for whatever gains are possible. Those people with an entrepreneurial spirit are like animals, blessed to have no time and no ability to think about the ways things should be, or how they'd prefer them to be."

COVID-19 presented a set of constraints unlike anything we ever could have imagined. In the nine years the physical studio has been open, we've maybe been closed a total of nine days - only major holidays. It was inconceivable to even consider closing for three days, let alone weeks at a time. COVID-19 forced us to make decisions and move quickly. We had to figure out how to work within the parameters of the mandatory shut down, yet we also knew people would need the benefits of the practice in order to deal with the stress and uncertainty during this unprecedented time. Instead of trying to change reality, we looked at how we could operate within the constraints of the given system. We were able to pivot and move online within eight hours of closing our physical doors.

Sometimes in order to grow into what's next, either as an individual or as a business, you just have to take the leap of faith. We had been working on moving things online for five years, yet COVID-19 forced us to make that move literally overnight. Even when we felt we weren't ready, even when we were still building technology and refining processes. And it worked.

Often the best route through any problem is straight through the middle. It can be messy, there may be some uncomfortable moments, but yoga teaches us to relax with what is, to find ease in the moment. One breath at a time. People experience overwhelm when they get too far ahead of themselves. Just take the next step, then the next one, and keep on going. Trust that the right people and tools will come into your life at just the right moment. Trust that those seemingly mundane, or uninspiring moments are essential for your later success. Keep asking, "What lesson can I learn here" and "How can I use this in my life for business?" or "How might this be useful to help another person?" Any experience in your life, even the unthinkable, can be a gift if you decide it is.

About four years ago I had a client, J.R. She lost her eight-year-old son in a horrible car accident. I remember noticing in our email reports that she had opened our messages, so I thought I'd reach out directly and invite her to come to yoga. Was it the magic cure to unimaginable pain? No, but it was the tool I had to offer. She came into the studio the next week. A friend drove her, as she couldn't bring herself to operate a vehicle after the accident. When she arrived at the studio, her grief was palpable. She kept coming regularly. She said it was the only place she would go other than her house. The studio was a safe place where she could feel the pain and grief in her body and let it come up. There was nothing to "do" about it. No shoving it down or trying to "transform" it; she would just allow it to come up and process out of her body. One day when she came in she told me she was just feeling so sad. As I told her, "You won't be the first person to cry in here in a yoga pose…. sad is what you are supposed to be right now. Let it come up and allow it to be." The way I see it, it's sort of like digestion. If you eat a big meal, your body has to digest the food. It can absorb and assimilate what is useful and then move the waste out of your body. The same thing has to happen with emotions; they have to be processed and moved out.

Little by little, J.R. began to heal; the pain no longer gripping and glimpses of joy began to emerge. I ran into her a few months ago at my daughter's school; she was barely recognizable. Her face was lighter, and there was a vibrancy about her. She told me she had another baby, born exactly two years to the date of the accident. She was able to reframe the accident in a way that was empowering. She went on to tell me about the non-profit she had formed to help other parents who had lost their kids in tragic accidents. Had J.R. not lost her son, she never would have been in a position to help others. There is always a gift in any situation, but you have to look for it.

During the school shut down for COVID-19, my daughter, Kathryn, was able to launch The Bright Podcast. She ranked in the top 100 for Entrepreneurism. At 14 years old! COVID-19 gave her the gift of uninterrupted time with no school work or outside activities. As much as she was disappointed about missing out on several trips we had planned, she was able to move beyond the disappointment, work with the existing circumstances to turn it into something positive. We continue to use the gift of COVID-19 to expand our online offerings and reach clients who have moved out of the area, as well as new clients from around the world. The personalized instruction in our live, online studio provides health and vitality you just can't get from YouTube.

One of our clients, Joann, a Chicago-based critical care doctor, who cares for infants born to COVID+ mothers, reported that her yoga practice allowed her to find beauty and peace in the midst of sickness and sadness of her patients. Joann has been known to join online classes from the "on-call" room at the hospital in her scrubs.

We know that this practice has a ripple effect. Brenleigh, one of our clients and a 3rd grade teacher, said she joined EPIC for lower back problems but what she got and continues to get goes beyond helping her back pain. She said, "the inclusive, positive atmosphere at EPIC, along with the mindfulness centered practice, has changed me. It has helped me develop a more forgiving and complete sense of self and has equipped me with self-regulating and mind opening practices. I am a teacher, and I started incorporating things I learned at EPIC into my daily routine with my third graders. Everyday, we had five to ten minutes of mindfulness where we engaged in yoga poses, guided visualization, and breathwork. We loved this time together to refocus, unwind, and get in touch with ourselves in the midst of a crazy day. The impact of EPIC is not only on the members who attend classes, but on everyone who comes into contact with the members because the change in mindset and world view is contagious and influential."

The idea that we can impact children through a teacher taking on online class is priceless. Studies have shown yoga increased the GPA of middle schoolers 2.7%. Also reported was increased focus and attention and down regulation of the sympathetic nervous system. Kids were able to increase vagal nerve tone, which led to the ability to better self-regulate.

We've heard that this practice challenges people in ways beyond the physical practice. Eve Overland, a Celebrity Personal Trainer, who regularly works with Carrie Underwood said, "Leanne and the EPIC community helped me realize what I needed most, especially at that time in my life. I found community. I found the ability to give myself grace. I found ease in effort. I could slow my busy mind and body down. I could breathe. And, I heard these words that impacted my life on a grander scale and put things into perspective: "The world does not see you, the way YOU see you". This was a game changer."

Yoga opens people up to what's possible in both their bodies and in life. These practices impact people in many different ways. From moms like Angela who said, "Teacher training restored my confidence after years of being a stay-at-home mom. I loved yoga but never dreamed I could teach it. I am not one to speak up in large groups unless it is my family or close group of friends, so leading strangers in a yoga class was way out of my comfort zone. One of the biggest rewards was deciding to quit my anxiety medication the day I graduated from teacher training. EPIC yoga teacher training was so much more than teaching poses... it was fuel for the soul."

As we continue to expand our reach, it's clear the hybrid online-brick and mortar model is here to stay. People love the convenience of being at home while maintaining connection with the EPIC community. Our Members have also appreciated having access to our Member's Portal with additional practices, meditations, guest interviews and other tools for optimal health and wellness. Health is no longer merely defined as fitness, but rather balanced body, mind and spirit.

We have been able to share yoga with different populations, from middle school students, to young adults aging out of the foster care system, to people who have suffered a traumatic brain injury, to people from the slums of Africa. Regardless of their circumstances, the practice works. Seven years ago I went to Africa to assist a yoga training program led by Baron Baptiste and Paige Elenson for Africa Yoga Project. Africa Yoga Project trains teachers and provides them with a living wage by teaching yoga to people who otherwise would not have access. Many of the participants were from the informal settlements outside Nairobi.

During that trip, I got to meet Leah, who I had been mentoring online for the last five years. As I spent time with Leah and her family, I was reminded that we are all more alike than different. However the one thing that struck me is that laughter seemed to be more prevalent. As I was leaving Nairobi, it was clear to me that I had lost touch with joy. Sometimes we get so caught up in the pursuit of dollars or success that we forget to live. I think a million-dollar life isn't based on dollars; it's based on your contributions to your family and your legacy. You don't have to go to Africa to have the experience of a lifetime. You could have it right at home. Sometimes we want to make such a big impact that we forget to impact the people who are in our homes. I think it is important to serve the people right in front of you.

Trust that the impact you make is big enough, that you are enough.

For more information about EPIC or Leanne, check out:

https://epicyogacenter.com/

https://epicyogaonline.com/

Or her podcast, The EPIC Journey

Live inspired!

Leanne

Kathryn Woehlke

WHAT'S THE RIGHT AGE TO BEGIN YOUR DREAM?

Kathryn Woehlke, Teen Entrepreneur, Podcast Host of The Bright Podcast and CEO of Bright Industries.
(www.brightpodcast.net)

> *"Use your smile to change the world, don't let the world change your smile."*
>
> Connor Franta

Both of my parents are so incredibly loving and supportive while still being so strong. I think that having role models that I could watch being so confident, loving, supporting and powerful at the same time has really helped me to become the kind of person I am today, which ultimately is the main reason I've had any success at all in entrepreneurship.

My mom is definitely one of the people that helped shape

me the most, just from seeing all the things she's been able to accomplish through hard work. About four months after I was born, my dad got cancer, and then after the doctors *thought* they had cured him, it came back. Instead of just accepting the unacceptable, she decided to take matters into her own hands. Even though she was wearing herself thin taking care of the two of us, she persevered. She researched, implemented, and fought for what she knew, starting to dive head first into health and wellness. She would take me in my stroller to the bookstore and read every book she could find on cancer, nutrition, or anything even remotely related to wellness. She started juicing, meditating, "all the things." Even though it seemed a little crazy at first, no one could deny the amazing results she was getting. Eventually, my dad started to get better, and now 14 years later, he is completely cured, which my mom likes to credit to all her green juice "concoctions" (which we all somehow got addicted to in the process.) Although I am a vegetarian and don't eat meat, I'll drink a carrot, apple, garlic juice any day of the week.

Later on, when I was starting kindergarten, my mom decided to finally open her yoga studio, EPIC Yoga. A lot of the people there actually know me by name because I was always up there helping with something or just hanging out. Being up there, even if it was only doing little tasks, I think helped to serve as a starting point to get me into business and entrepreneurship.

One of my biggest influences is also my dad. He's always been super sharp; we call him "wikidadia," sort of like "wikipedia." You can ask him anything about just about any subject and he will launch into all kinds of facts and knowledge. He started a joint venture company, reaching $1 Billion in 99 days. At the time I didn't recognize the success (I was two years old), but looking back on it now, it shows me the success someone can accomplish. It was a lot of work, and some late nights that I know he wishes he was home, but the hard work was so rewarding for him and our family. Seeing someone so close to me be successful helped me believe that I, too, can be successful. My parents' accomplishments and their mindset for success leads to their supporting me and my big dreams. I think of it sort of like achieving my "four minute mile" in business. I say that because people used to think that running a four minute mile couldn't be done, that it was just not humanly possible. Apparently they were wrong, because on May 6th, 1954, Roger Banister did the seemingly impossible and broke the four minute mile, and the belief that went with it, because soon, more and more people were following in his footsteps and doing the supposedly impossible. In my opinion, I think that so many people just accepted that was something that no one could do, so they never really tried, but once Bannister had done it, they saw him and thought, "*Well, if he could, so can I!*"

That's what my parents were for me, showing me that doing the "impossible," and making their dreams become living, breathing, <u>real</u>, realities is totally possible. That's what I'm hoping I can be for so many other people. I want you to see that you don't need tons of experience, a bunch of degrees, a ton of cash, time, or to give up your life in the process. But, with a mission, a road map, and hard work, you can do this! (And if you're going to listen to anything I say, listen to this: TRUST ME, if *I* can do this, you most definitely can!)

I know that that wasn't exactly my backstory, but I think in order to truly understand "my" backstory, you need to know a little about the people that helped shape me into the person I've become today. Okay, here is a little bit about me…

Hi, I'm Kathryn Woehlke, I'm the host of The Bright Podcast and CEO of Bright Industries. www.brightpodcast.net. For the most part of my life, I was never exactly sure what my answer was to the question everyone seemed to ask, "What do you want to be when you grow up?" What you know (hopefully if you actually read any of those random words I typed out in the beginning of this thing) is that I grew up immersed in the business world so I knew I wanted to make a difference, I wanted to be remembered, and I wanted to help people, somehow. I wasn't sure if I was going to put together and run giant companies like my dad, create a business specifically to help people, like my mom, or make some giant discovery like the marine biology dreams the universe had been whispering in my ear since I was little.

Eventually, I knew I was going into marine biology, one way or another, but I felt I wanted something more. Studying the ocean is great, and I loved the idea, but I was still longing for some way to make an impact, to make my mark on the world. Later, I just reached a point of acceptance, "I'll do marine biology, and figure the rest out later," but I didn't want to wait till later, or leave that all up to chance. (I"ll admit, the people that know me *know* I'm not a very patient person.)

I just went through my life as normal, I did well in school, hung out with my friends, played volleyball, and just let things run their course. Sports were definitely one of the first things to really push me, even as I switched between so many of them. Volleyball was one of the ones that I really loved. I think because it was where I was challenged the most. My awesome coaches (mostly) challenged me to truly give my all, not only on the court, but for everything I did in life.

About a year and a half ago, my mom decided to take a chance on these things called "funnels." When I first heard her talk about this I thought she was talking about the little plastic things you use to pour stuff. Nope. It was business stuff. One of her friends told her to go to this event called Funnel Hacking Live. Her friend told her, "You'll get at least one thing out of it if you go," so she figured, "Why not?" Towards the end of the event, during the pitch for Russell Brunson's coaching group, Two Comma Club X, she was "SOLD!" as she told me, when he started talking about having an event for families to bring their kids to. She had been wanting me to understand a little bit more about this whole business "thing." She saw an opportunity, and took it, which looking back now, was one of the best decisions she could've made. Once she got home, she started to try to teach me about all of this "funnely" stuff she had learned, and all the amazing people she had met, but to be honest, I was perfectly cool with my friends and Netflix without some weird new thing that seemed to me more like a cult then a coaching group. (Don't worry, there's nothing cult-like about it.) I started to *slowly* come around a little bit, letting her tell me some of what she had found out, but honestly, I was doing it more for her good than mine.

Later on, my mom decided to take me to an event called Unlock The Secrets, which was basically a kid version of Click-Funnel's event Funnel Hacking Live. I was more excited to get out of school, then whatever she was taking me to. My Dad and I were planning on finding other things to go do while my mom went to "her funnel conference thing," but somehow, again, she persuaded us to at least give it a real chance.

Once we got there, she took me to one of Jamie Atkinson's podcasting masterminds. I figured I was just going to sit and go on my phone or something. Because quite frankly, I had no idea what was going on. I was *wayyy* out of my league, but then things started changing. I was actually "getting" what they were saying. When there was something I didn't understand, I started to take notes on my phone. I shared it with my mom, literally some of the fastest words I'd ever typed. I was typing questions into that note as fast as my fingers could go, and with friends that text as fast as mine do, that's definitely saying something. Even though I was getting most of what these people were saying, I still felt like I was way out of my league. As my mom and I were furiously typing in this note, I had an epiphany, an idea that I could basically "see." It was as clear as the Denver view through the windows next to us.

I had questions I wanted to ask, but I just didn't know if people would listen to them, considering I was a "kid" and totally new to ALL of this. Eventually, my mom, being who she is, forced me to ask the questions myself. She informed me via the apple note, which I'm now realizing was not nearly as discreet as we thought, or hoped.

Once I actually started to speak up and share my thoughts, things started to get really real, really fast. I was so nervous that I was going to be seen as the person who "didn't belong in the room," but it was the exact opposite. Once I started talking, the conversation almost never stopped. These people not only took me seriously, probably more so than I did, but they were giving me feedback, agreeing with me, and helping me turn this idea into a real, tangible thing, something that I might actually be able to do. That was definitely one of the first experiences I had in the entrepreneurship arena, outside of the bubble I had at home.

People were believing and *listening to* what I was saying, much to my surprise (trust me!) Throughout that event, everything kind of started to snowball. I was getting more confident, talking to more and more people, just sharing what I had to say, and people wanted to listen. I was talking to more people, giving opinions, and becoming more confident in what I wanted to do - even getting people, who had just presented on stage and taught me these concepts, to agree to come on my podcast.

I knew how much this event helped me, through the people I'd met and the things I'd learned, and I felt driven to share this with other people.

I knew these concepts and the motivation from the speakers needed to get out in the world. This was the information "kids"\other young people like me, needed to hear. That's why I decided to start The Bright Podcast, so that other kids who didn't weren't exposed to the kinds of experiences I was, could get the same knowledge and opportunities.

I have seen people let their dreams die because they weren't sure how to get them out into the world. Maybe they didn't have the connections to find someone that did, or maybe they just didn't have someone who believed in them. I wanted to change that. I want to show kids that their voices do matter, and I wanted to give them a way to share their message. That event helped me to become more confident, experienced, and finally have a roadmap for my dreams.

That event and those people altered the course of my life. They helped me realize that I can become who I want to be, and that's what I want for other people, too. I want to help other people realize that you can create a profitable company without waiting for a college degree or needing a ton of experience, time, or cash. You don't have to wait until you are an adult or some other arbitrary time point to share your bright idea with the world.

Through my podcast, I want to help share the tips and tools of super successful entrepreneurs. It's my hope that each episode will provide insight and inspiration that people may not otherwise hear.

I plan to keep learning about the smart way to do entrepreneurship and sharing it with kids through my podcast, course, and other outlets. As the world changes, I plan to keep learning and sharing with my audience so that we can make a meaningful contribution to the world and make it better.

I intend to use my entrepreneurial skills to fund the things I'm passionate about and make a difference. I hope to start a charity to support ocean exploration and preservation after college, but I will educate myself before then because I don't feel like I need to wait until college to begin my life.

The goal of my entire entrepreneurial journey isn't really anything special - nothing genius, revolutionary or brilliant. I'm just trying to provide the inspiration, tools and path to help people get a little closer to their dreams and create profitable companies they love so they can live the life they want. There are so many people who live a life with regrets and missing out on their "bucket list." This whole "Bright" movement is about giving people the tools and inspiration to live the life they want while doing what they actually love.

A lot of people go about this the wrong way, thinking I'll be happy once I've made this much money, or that success equals money. I'm going to let you in on a little secret; money isn't the destination, or at least the right one. So many people get stuck in this cycle of, "I need to work this job I hate to pay for this car," and "I need this car to get to this job," thinking that's the way to success.

Money is really just a tool you can use to grow your business, not the thing you actually want. Almost everyone, who does things solely for the money, says the money doesn't bring happiness. If you aren't going to enjoy the journey, what's the point of wasting all that time to get to a destination only to repeat the cycle, never really fulfilled?

That's not to say that money is a bad thing, not at all!

Money is a TOOL, not a measure of success. It's a resource to help you get to where you want to go, to live the life you want and help the people you can, NOT the destination.

When talking to successful entrepreneurs, the ONE thing they all emphasized was the importance of mindset. Mindset is your mental attitude. It's those thoughts you tell yourself automatically, the constant narrative in your head. In order to be truly successful, you have to believe it. Doubts can derail you before you even begin.

The common denominator in many success stories is a positive mental attitude. Successful people go all in!

One of the problems I've seen when people start a business, or anything else, is that they're afraid of failure! Fear can paralyze people before they even begin the race. There's a process called "failing forward" which means as long as you learn from your failures and keep moving forward, you are making progress. Failure is kind of like a revision process for your business, constantly helping you find ways to improve and make it better. Failing is actually, despite what most people think, an advantage, if you treat it as such. Many people give up because they're scared of "What if this won't work," or "What will people think?" and that is what separates so many of the great success stories from the failures in today's world.

People can also get stuck on the idea that what they have to share isn't relevant, or revolutionary, not something people want or will need to hear. When actually everyone has something they're good at that, if you share it with people, it could improve their lives in some way, big or small.

So many other people give up because they think that they can't make a profitable company doing what they love, or something they're passionate about, when there is not one idea I've ever heard (yet) that didn't have a successful company hiding behind it. If you're passionate about what you're doing, and want to be able to share it with the world, you'll therefore be more likely to have an amazing product or service. If you think your amazing product or service can help people, you'll be more inclined to share it with the people you want to help. If the people you're trying to help see you're genuine, and not just in it for the money, they'll be more likely to buy from you and share what you have to say, because they know you're doing what you're doing for the right reasons, and if you keep doing that, you're company is going to spread like WILDFIRE

(during a tornado!!)

Another one of the key things to having a good mindset is accountability. When there's someone there to hold you accountable, or people that are waiting for you to follow through on something you've promised, you're so much less likely to bail or let failure win. Even for me, starting my podcast, it took wayyy longer than it should have, because I didn't have the right mindset. I knew what I wanted to tell people, I knew people wanted to hear it, but I was also so worried about things like, "What will people think?" or "What if this doesn't work," or "What if people don't take me seriously?" I already had a lot on my plate, with my last year of middle school, travel volleyball, my friends, and having to find some time to sleep in there. Once people started asking to be interviewed, or I asked people to be interviewed, I knew I couldn't just keep procrastinating. I had people counting on me! So I finally just did it, and it really paid off, ranking in multiple countries, including the US, and getting to be ranked in categories with amazing people like Gary Vaynerchuk and Russell Brunson!

One of the questions I get asked the most often is from parents, wondering how to get their kids into entrepreneurship, or how to help them along, and my answer is almost always the same. You can't force this on somebody or trust me, it just won't work. When my mom tried to get me more into entrepreneurship and business, I stayed far away with Netflix and my friends, because it wasn't something I wanted to do at that time. If you try to force this on anyone, even though everyone can do it, it just won't work. Your kids will never love it, never have fun with it, and never stick with it.

I think parents just need to help their kids find what they are passionate about, and be there to support. It may not be exactly the kind of thing you thought they would do at first, but you just need to be there and support them, not try to change or control what they want to do. And parents, when you are invested and trying to help, without trying to form things the way you want them (no matter how much you may want to,) it's going to help so much more than you can imagine.

The last thing, my main point, (honestly if you just remember this you're going to be golden), the main thing if you want to start a business - you just need to make sure you're believing in what you're doing. Have the confidence in yourself that you *can* do it, your idea *is* going to work. (And don't worry - I know how cliche this sounds.) Just believe in yourself and go all in, and you'll get where you want to go SO much faster. Even if you fail, don't let that take away your amazing idea! Now you know what went wrong with that attempt, and you can focus *now* on how to take what you now know doesn't work, and apply that to your next idea. That try may have failed, but that doesn't mean it was a *failure*. There were still good things there, good things you can carry over to make the next time you try your idea more and more successful! You can't keep focusing on what went wrong, or you might miss the next golden opportunity. Those bad parts of your idea aren't necessarily bad, too, you just have to try looking at them from a different angle, reevaluating and figuring out *why* they may have not gone like you wanted them to, then use that to make your next idea even better. Then, without a doubt, you'll get wherever you want to go in life.

(Honestly if you've made it this far, congrats! I'm not quite sure how you listened to me ramble for that long, I don't know if I could do it, but hopefully you got something out of that mess of words, that can help make sure you get wherever you're trying to go, and live an amazing fulfilled life!)

Be Bright!

www.brightpodcast.net

Kathryn

Holly Homer

HOW CAN YOU CRAFT THE LIFE YOU WANT?

*Holly Homer, CEO, Holly Homer Enterprises
(KidsActivities.com)*

> *"Do the best you can until you know better. Then when you know better, do better."*
>
> Maya Angelou

I am not a technical person. My husband used to download my emails for me, which I now realize was him just opening my email, but that's how crazy low-tech I am. I can change a light bulb, but don't expect me to do anything beyond that. Even using the remote control is a challenge. That makes it even more outstanding to describe myself as someone in technology. It all started for me around 14 years ago.

I had three little boys all under the age of five. It was

an intense situation for me. I had spent time in corporate America. I have a Master's degree in physical therapy. I was a rehab director at one of the top pain clinics in the country. When I went to my job, I had employees, I went to committee meetings, I would write policy, and people would listen to me. I would speak on workers' compensation in the workplace and people were paying attention to what I had to say.

I realized that I had always wanted to be a stay-at-home mom, so I left my job. It went well at first because when you have one or two kids, they're portable. You can still get out and see the world. Somewhere between the second and third kid, the dynamics of what you're able to do changes. This is especially true if they're little.

It started on a Saturday morning. My husband's a doctor and always at work. There's an unbelievable amount of chaos that three little boys can cause in your life.

My friend Jodi was a good friend from college who I hadn't seen in years and we reconnected over email. She had two little boys the same age as my older ones, so we shared this feeling of not being alone in the world. We'd write these long emails to each other every Saturday morning. Those helped me get through the day until bedtime.

We could sympathize with each other because we were going through the same things. That Saturday, I'd sent her an email and was waiting for her response. I waited and waited and waited... until I realized it wasn't coming.

I thought to myself, "I need this today more than ever." When the email arrived, I was surprised that the subject line was **I think we should stop emailing.** It freaked me out. I opened up the email, and she said:

Hey, I am emailing with another person as I do with you. And I just figured out that we can all start blogs and then we wouldn't have to email each other. We could just go and read each other's blogs.

She continued with, "Go to blogspot.com and just fill out the form and that will get you a blog." I went immediately. I filled out the form, and it asked for the name of the blog. What came to me at that moment was June Cleaver Nirvana.

I became a blogger that day. It was funny because I started my blog without ever reading a blog, knowing what a blog was, or seeing anyone else's blog. At first, I patterned my blog posts after my emails to Jodi, but then realized that I could upload photos. Uploading photos was revolutionary because it gave me the ability to share pictures of the boys with relatives instead of creating multiple versions of scrapbooks for each person.

Scrapbooking was expensive! Blogging was going to save me a ton of money.

That's how this started for me. I put these stories and pictures online and let everyone I know, including Jodi, my mom, and my aunt. It was going to be amazing.

About three weeks in, I was posting on my blog and I noticed that I had a comment from someone who wasn't my mom or Jodi. Her name was Megan, and her name was written in a distinct color. I clicked on her name and discovered that Megan had a blog.

It took me by surprise when I found out that other people blog, too!

Megan had a blogroll on the sidebar of her blog. I went crazy because I had found a bunch of people just like me on that list. It was a bunch of moms who were talking just like me! We were talking about what we were doing every day.

Many of those bloggers I discovered on Megan's blogroll are still my friends today. What had started as a need for adult conversation and a scrapbooking replacement turned into the community that I craved.

Fast forward several years. I wanted to recreate a place for my readers like the one that had been so helpful for me. A place where we can feel comfortable - where we're surrounded by positive, supportive moms.

I hope that KidsActivities.com has become that place.

And it all started by accident.

That's a common theme throughout my entire business. I think one thing is that when you do something—when you take action with no expectation—whatever comes next is all accidental but it's supposed to happen. By putting additional effort into it, you build it up and put a foundation underneath it on purpose. I think we're in a time in the world where we're making things up as we go.

When you look at the journey of the early bloggers it becomes apparent that we simply made it up as we went along. We couldn't Google how to start a blog. Those search results did not exist. We were making our own path. It's harder to start these things today because there are expectations of what everything is supposed to look like. Why not take out those expectations and see where everything leads? That's a much better business plan for many people.

You can't do it if you're comparing what you're doing today

with what I've been doing for 15 years. I mean, if I wasn't doing something a little different, that would be a problem. I've learned something.

Hi, my name is Holly Homer, and I'm the CEO of Holly Homer Enterprises. I run KidsActivities.com (or Kids Activities Blog) and the Quirky Momma Facebook page. I have had the opportunity to write three books because of my blog and they have sold over 215K copies.

The main point of Holly Homer Enterprises is to provide all the resources parents need for kids activities. We stress traditional play and make it about the process rather than the result.

Real life mothering was something that wasn't being seen at that time. You would open a Pottery Barn kids catalog and see the suggested little boy's room decorated in light colors and perfectly orderly except for a wooden train askew on the floor. If they came to my house, they'd see a far different picture. They'd see a billion Lego pieces on the floor and chaos.

I've created a place where moms can be okay with both the order and the chaos.

Let's have activities that make a difference and help us bond with our kids. If your kid wants to play with Legos for hours, do it with them. Find things that you can do with your kids in those 'throwaway' minutes. For instance, what can you do while you're waiting in line? What can you do when you're in a doctor's waiting room?

It's in those throwaway moments that memories are being made with our kids. It's in those moments when the relationship with our kids are being strengthened. I wanted a way to celebrate that online.

It's really cool to help other moms with the opportunity to earn money from home. They can work either part-time or full-time doing what I was doing when my kids were little. My business continues to grow from my living room with very little overhead.

Now I teach others to leverage that to a level that can support their family or at least bring in some extra money every month. One of my favorite things about the business is the opportunity that people have from just being part of my company. That's exciting for me.

You know, there's very little stability these days. Your business has to be sustainable - able to cover its costs both in money and your time. Creating that sustainability is the first goal as a business. The second goal as a business is always to try new things.

I'm always looking for the latest trends and what's new. Where are people congregating online? How are things changing, and what does it look like? When Oprah had her show about vision boards, she asked everyone to write out where they would be in a year and where they would be in five years.

I remember thinking, "I haven't a clue." What I'll be doing in five years probably hasn't been invented yet. When I approach what I do today with that in mind, it doesn't mean that I'm not headed in a direction. It just means that I'm open to what those new possibilities might be.

One of the most important lessons I've learned happened early in my physical therapy life when I was the Rehab Director at one of the top pain clinics in the country. I worked for two brilliant doctors that ran the clinic. One of them was specifically in charge of the money. When they first hired me, I told them they had a great clinic, but I needed a specific piece of equipment that I'd had at my last few clinics. The doctor nodded, but it was clear he was only paying half attention to me.

Weeks passed by, and I still didn't have that piece of equipment. It was expensive, not something that we would easily write a check for. I went back to the doctor and pleaded with him for this piece of equipment. And nothing happened.

I go back to him a month later. I'm begging him, and he finally noticed me. He said, "Holly, show me the numbers." It was then that I learned you can win any argument with numbers.

I came back to him with the cost, explained how we would pay it off and the amount. I showed him the increased amount we can charge patients, and how we'll be able to treat patients faster. I handed the numbers to him, and he signed the check that day! I've learned since then that numbers solve everything.

One of the magical things about running an online business is that there are numbers associated with everything we do.

When you look at your online numbers, it's like peering behind the scenes and asking, "What did people vote for today?" It becomes very clear what your next step needs to be. Every Facebook post that we put up on Quirky Momma is an election of sorts. Is this something you want to see more of? Is this something you want to see less of? Every single engagement - a comment, like, or a share - all goes into that kind of voting process.

If you think of testing as a mini-experiment, it helps your ego to deal with any failures. They're not failures. It's data that shows you what your people want or don't want. If you look at your numbers consistently, you will quickly become an expert on your numbers.

When I speak, I have a slide that shows all the blogs and major projects I've started through the last 15 years. There are 17 of them on that slide. On the next slide, there are big X's on everything that didn't work out. 15 of the 17 blogs and major projects I have started have a big X on them. I have failed majorly a high percentage of the time!

But the truth is, each of those 15 failures was an education. Each taught me something that I am able to leverage today in my successful business. The fastest path to learning something is through trying it. Yes, even if it fails.

What's so funny about this online universe is that we think we have this window into people's worlds. You might judge yourself based on a beautiful, harmonious picture that I post of my family on Facebook. But what you don't see is the 15 failed projects or the 32 terrible pictures that led up to that one success. And you might not suspect that I had to bribe my kids with hundreds of dollars to get that picture. That's the part of the story you never see.

In every single one of those projects that went down in

flames, there was some lesson I was supposed to learn that makes me a better person today.

I have learned to get over myself. And then I re-learn that lesson at least once a week! My friend, Lori Turk, is one of my mentors. She always says, "You know, learn the lesson the first time or it will just keep being presented to you over and over again until you learn it." I think of her every single time I am presented the opportunity to learn to get over myself... again.

We have to be able to give ourselves space, the ability to move, and the permission to pivot. Embrace the freedom to fail. I'm no longer scared of failing because I've done it so often! I've been there, done that, and I am still standing.

We're brought up in an education system where we're graded regularly. We're told that if you do something how someone else wants you to do it, you get an A+. That's a tough path that you're putting in front of yourself.

If you read about the movers and shakers in our world's history, whether that be in politics or business, you'll discover clear and original ideas. These people never sat in the front row and correctly answered all the questions.

In fact, Andrew Carnegie, one of America's richest men, in an interview with Napoleon Hill, the author of *Think and Grow*

Rich, said back in the 1920's, that one burden he had on his heart for today's youth is that they blindly follow authority. I think today that's even truer, because part of what has happened in modernizing society is that we've become more uniform, we've bought into groupthink. We've become more likely to follow the leader.

You absolutely have to get out of that pattern when you are an entrepreneur. If you're always following, you will never get started. If you're always waiting for someone to tell you what to do, your business will never grow.

You also have to be okay with the thousand times that you do something and nothing happens. All of your actions are compounding, and the only way to gain this knowledge is to do it yourself. Try it out. Learn from people who've gone before you but be willing to adapt it and make it your own.

One of the biggest obstacles I see in the mindset of today's entrepreneur is that they need to be taught something instead of trying to do it themselves. Get into the trenches and figure out what you don't know. If you eventually need to learn some part of that process, you will be better prepared to learn and more importantly, understand what information you still lack. We must become independent and step into leadership roles, even if it doesn't come naturally. It is the only way our business will move forward.

Don't be afraid to adjust your course based on your experience. It will happen naturally! I had an unexpected shift in my business that worked out really well. I wrote June Cleaver Nirvana about me and the boys. You know, potty training, allowances, boys fighting, home chaos and all the thought processes I have as a mother.

My blog was telling the world, "Hey, this is how I'm approaching motherhood and I'm not necessarily an expert, but it's what I wanted and I think I'm doing an okay job and hopefully I'll be able to make enough money to pay for their therapy down the road." I was giving a peek into our lives daily.

That worked really well, and I had a lot of fun with that and the blog got some traction. I started having readers. That traction was evident when I was picking up my boys in the car line at school and a teacher said, "Oh, Holly, that was so funny what you wrote yesterday about that child."

And it just hit me: There's a point in this journey where your stories are no longer yours.

My stories were no longer my stories. Those stories belonged to my children. It was up to them if they were ever to be told.

That's when I shifted during that process from the personal blog to purchasing the site, Quirky Momma (now KidsActivities.com) from another blogger. One reason I did that was I saw she had started this blog where she was just writing, not about the kids, not about the stories, but about the things they were doing together.

It was a new idea that I had never thought about before because in my mind, the only ones who did projects were people like Martha Stewart, who spent hundreds of dollars to put them together. Nobody had really done that for the mom opening the kitchen junk drawer.

This was a way I could still create that community without jeopardizing my children's stories and without my children being completely embarrassed.

My children, for as long as they have been alive and can remember, have been the children of a blogger. I've tried not to embarrass them in public, but I've failed at that. They're used to seeing mom with a camera, telling the story.

One time, I put dinner on the table and nobody lifted their forks to eat. I asked, "Are you guys going to eat?" And they asked me, "Well, have you taken the pictures?"

I wondered whether I was living my life for the pictures or I was living my life and taking pictures of it. It was a struggle early on. There are things that I get excited about that I would never put on my blog or tell anyone about. Those are my secrets.

For instance, one thing I would never do is take on a travel sponsor because I don't want my vacation to become work. There is a clear separation now between those moments that I would never, ever write about; those are mine and the rest would go on the blog.

I want you to trust yourself. You are smart and know what you are doing. One thing I see over and over again with my coaching clients is that they second-guess their brilliance. It's one reason why I love coaching. A lot of times we'll sit down together and a client will say, "This is what I think I need to do." And I'll say, "That's actually what you need to do!"

It can be nice to have confirmation. Running an online business is often a lonely place without a lot of affirmation from others.

One of my recent clients has an amazing blog that is followed faithfully by many. She already had traffic, interaction on social media and an uplifting community. She was trying to sell these adorable mini recipe books with different themes for between $1 and $4. They were amazing products that change how you put dinner on the table. Each one of them solved a little problem and yet they weren't selling. When I asked her why she thought they weren't selling, she told me she hadn't put them in front of her readers as much as she should.

I completely agreed. One thing that consumer research shows is that some people need to see something seven times before they consider the purchase. She wasn't giving them the opportunity!

She already had the email list, social media following and blog traffic and she had a great product. We just needed to get them together and then repeat over and over.

But one of the reasons she had held back was because she doubted herself. There hadn't been a rush of sales when she first put them out into the world. She interpreted that as disinterest in the product even wondering if people just didn't like them.

I asked her, "What would happen if you don't sell any of these products? What's the downside of implementing this plan?" What was the absolute worst case scenario? Maybe you spend time promoting the products over and over and have just a handful of sales. When you think about it that way, there's no downside. It's not like you get your email list, social media following and readership taken away because you present this amazing solution to your community's problems and they decide not to buy it.

I absolutely love being the voice of confirmation in my coaching relationships. I reassure my clients that our businesses are not that breakable. And, if we are tinkering, it can be very beneficial in the long run because of the data we collect.

For instance, If we implement this plan and you sell zero, then we're ahead of the game because now we know what doesn't work. Now the truth is, when she implemented her plan, she sold hundreds.

We are not promised tomorrow, so how can we make today awesome? I just wanted adult conversation 15 years ago. That was the only thing that I was craving, and it led me to give myself permission to try a bunch of new things. A bunch of new things that I was terrible at in the beginning.

There is a quote from Garrett White that I love: "You're going to suck, you're going to suck real bad at first. What you're going to find over time though is that eventually you're going to suck less. And, eventually, you might even get to the point where you're actually good."

People are always under pressure, having to make new

decisions on the fly. They're also being presented with fresh opportunities that maybe they would not have given themselves permission to consider before. What I ask of you is that you look at opportunities as just opportunities rather than lifelong commitments. Try things on for size for a little while and see how they fit.

If I hadn't started the blog because I was so desperate for adult conversation, if I hadn't been so desperately a hot mess, it wouldn't have led to the next thing and the next thing and the next thing... I've learned that if we can step back to a certain extent, we can figure out how to wrangle the chaos.

I think any mom can identify with wrangling the chaos of any given moment. We have a choice to either leverage the chaos, ignore the chaos, or use the chaos as an opportunity for the future. I think what's super important today is to take today's chaos and leverage it.

Take whatever you have today and explore it a little further. It's literally like taking baby steps. My very favorite movie in the entire world is What About Bob? Because of that movie, everyday the day the mantra of "baby steps" goes through my mind. Bob tackled everything in life with just baby steps: baby steps to the elevator; baby steps to the sailboat; etc. It gives you permission to just do a little, a baby step, because as moms we have a lot going on.

We've got kids, we've got a house, we probably have a partner or husband. We have all that stuff and there's a lot of juggling. If you're not careful, it can take away from the magnitude of any given moment, or any given thing.

Just taking small steps forward adds up over time to a level that you could never have imagined when you started. Take that first step, whatever that looks like today. Even if you're going to back up and go in a different direction tomorrow, with that one step you will learn, and you will gather some data from that step that will help you down the road. You don't even know what that looks like.

If you're looking for something fun to do with your children, I encourage you to check out KidsActivities.com. I promise, there is some great adult-focused content on there, too! If you are looking for coaching to leverage data and your inner voice, check out HollyHomer.com. You got this even if you are clueless about what "this" looks like.

Holly

Epilogue

Now it's time for you to invest in yourself. Think of the offers, the collective wisdom represented in these chapters, and avail yourself of the compassion, heart, and experience of one or more of these humble and wise author-entrepreneurs. They have been where you are. They are here to serve so that you, in turn, may also serve - because the world really needs us right now! They are here to inspire you so that you, in turn, may inspire others to take action and turn your big dreams into reality.

As you've met the wonderful authors in this book - adults and young adults - reading their secrets of building businesses out of necessity or while still in school, I hope you have recognized some themes. Most of us thought we were headed one way only to have life throw us one or more curveballs, redirecting our paths significantly. Many of us tried to please others, or simply followed societal norms by going to school and pursuing a climb up the corporate ladder, only to finally appreciate what others tried to tell us; from a corporate standpoint, any individual employee's needs are irrelevant no matter how loyal you've been, how hard you've worked, or how many personal sacrifices you've made. Each of us has chosen to forego a paycheck in exchange for living intentionally and deliberately. Each of us is driven by our desire to make a difference, make an impact, and serve - and to do so has been a scary, uncomfortable, and deliberate choice to grow outside our comfort zones. As entrepreneurial parents, we give our kids the gift of choice. They don't have to follow our path but the option is definitely open to them to live life on their terms. We firmly believe that the more we step into who we are, who we serve, and why, the more our horizons expand and the more we find ourselves presented with new challenges. What's different now for each of us - and what each of us wants for you to feel - is that we believe 100% and more, that our big ginormous glorious dreams are possible. That we are possible! We are Million Dollar Moms and Million Dollar kids. We believe in our Million Dollar Stories and we believe you, too, are here to serve your readers and clients by using your unique experiences and expertise to offer them immediate relief, hope, and transformation because someone, somewhere, right now, is waiting desperately for YOU to provide a solution to their pain!

We are here to help you and to celebrate your journey. Thank you for sharing your time with us. If you found value in these stories, please take a minute and leave a review on Amazon - and tell a friend to buy this book. And of course, reach out to any of us about affiliate opportunities. Your Million Dollar Story begins with clarity and action. It is your time to act and it is your time to recognize *you are exactly where you are meant to be!*

My wish for you is that these stories nourish your belief, providing you with the courage to keep going in pursuit of your dreams - even if your dreams are forced in a new direction. I invite you to discover how collectively we, as these authors demonstrate, may use our unique stories and gifts - at ANY age - to change the world in small or large measure. These authors have also shown we can't do it alone. They want to help you so be sure you take advantage of all the links and resources provided to you in this book.

If you've read this far, know that you have your own special gift. You persevere. You care. You want more - for you, for your family, and for your tribe. And now you have ten new resources to help you make a difference and change lives.

Finally, if you haven't yet shared your story with the world, please don't wait much longer! If you are a Million Dollar Mom, a Million Dollar Realtor, a Million Dollar Network Marketer, a Million Dollar Dad, a Million Dollar Fitness champion…. It's time for you to craft and share *your* **Million Dollar Story!**

About the Authors

Kiana Danial

Kiana Danial, CEO of Invest Diva (www.investdiva.com), is an award-winning, internationally recognized personal investing and wealth management expert. Having been featured in The Wall Street Journal, TIME Magazine, Fox Business, CNNi, Forbes, TheStreet, Nasdaq, Cheddar, 77 WABC Radio and 710 WOR Radio, Kiana is a highly sought-after commentator, professional speaker and executive coach who delivers inspirational workshops and seminars to corporations, universities and entrepreneurial groups. Kiana has reported on the financial markets directly from the floor of the NYSE and NASDAQ, and was named the Personal Investment Expert of the Year in 2018 and the Investment Coach of the Year in 2019 by the Investment Fund Awards. An accomplished author, Kiana's books include 'Invest Diva's Guide to Making Money in Forex,' published by McGraw-Hill in 2013, and 'Cryptocurrency Investing For Dummies,' published by Wiley in 2019. Invest Diva's mission is to empower and educate women to take control of their financial future by investing in stocks and other online assets.

Chimene Van Gundy

Chimene Van Gundy is on a mission to help people explore passive income opportunities through investment in mobile homes and she is committed to changing lives and providing housing to as many people as possible. She has been recognized by Continental Who's Who as a Pinnacle Lifetime Achiever in the field of Real Estate as CEO and Founder of Outstanding Real Estate Solutions and Creator of the 'Mobile Home Millionaire' System. In 2016 Ms. Van Gundy was inducted into the International Rich Dad Hall of Fame and was the first entrepreneur to be featured on the cover of ICE (Inner Circle Executive) magazine which is usually reserved for CEO's and CFO's of Fortune 100 companies. Chimene serves as a featured writer for Think Realty magazine, where she educates others on the mobile home asset class, and she was featured in a collaborative book titled "Wealth for Women: Conversations with the Team That Creates the Dream - The Top Female Professionals Who Can Help You Get Wealthy in Real Estate." Additionally, she is a member of W.R.E.N. (Women's Real Estate Network.) where she was identified as one of the top 10 Female Real Estate Investors in the country. In December 2020, the International Association of Top Professionals (IAOTP) will be honoring Ms Van Gundy at its Annual Awards Gala being held at the Plaza Hotel in New York City. Also in 2020 she is being considered for a feature in TIP (Top Industry Professional) Magazine and will be broadcast on the famous Reuters Building in Times Square, NYC. Active in charitable work, Chimene is a donor to Guardians of the Children, Hill County Chapter, a local charity dedicated to educating the public on how to recognize and react to child abuse. And she has personally donated over six figures to Operation Underground Railroad, an organization that goes undercover around the world to save children from child sex trafficking.

In addition to being an author in *Million Dollar Moms*, she is being featured in an upcoming book with Melinda Gates, Jack Canfield, Oprah Winfrey, and other notable Americans.

Holly Homer

Holly is a professional blogger running Kids Activities Blog and the Quirky Momma FB page. She has used her blog and social media as a laboratory over the years to test all things traffic & algorithms. Holly is a best-selling author - her three books have sold over 215K copies. She has logged over 1000 hours on live video doing everything from teaching blogging, selling clothes, Crafting with Crap and opening oysters on the internet.

Bella Marsh

Bella Marsh is an up and coming young entrepreneur who has helped her mom make eight figures in her business. Her journey started soon after her mother's when she saw her mom repeatedly taken advantage of by those who were only in it for a quick profit. She decided to take action and use her wit and experience to help develop a course to teach others on how to wholesale mobile homes. Her goal in mind, similar to her mothers, was to help those less fortunate than others to find a way into the mobile homes industry, an untouched gold mine.

But not only that, to create a wave of investors that would soon help hundreds of others and provide affordable housing all around the world. Now she has taken her expertise to the next step in recent years and created a way to make money online on Amazon with minimal capital! She has even worked together with a teen homeless shelter to hopefully find a way to better their lives, excel in entrepreneurship and help them grow their self worth! Her goal with this business is to help others build a sustainable business online with minimal capital and help them get their first steps into entrepreneurship. She has used her past hardships and struggles to help those who need it through motivational speaking and opening up about the hardships on Social Media platforms. Her mission is to help inspire others and let them know that no matter what life throws at you that you are not alone and you can do anything you put your mind and heart to.

Alison J Prince

Alison J Prince has built four lucrative multimillion-dollar online businesses from the ground up. She's been featured in Forbes and on the cover of Costco Connection, but she feels her most successful business choice was teaching her 10- and 13-year-old daughters how to sell over $100,000 in products in just nine months. She watched them gain confidence, embrace entrepreneurship, and begin to live what she terms the "Because I Can" life.

While continuing to run her companies, Alison is also

committed to helping others achieve their financial goals. Through her successful 0-$100K System, she now teaches thousands how to create, launch, and grow profitable e-commerce businesses. Members of the BecauseICan Life appreciate her authentic, down-to-earth approach to business and life along with her constant encouragement that they have the ability to do whatever they put their minds to. Why? Because They Can.

Makayla Prince

Hey! It's Makayla. I'm a young entrepreneur who loves food, loves going on adventures, and hanging out with friends and family. When I was 13 I started my first business and that's when the entrepreneur bug bit! Since then I've started a few more businesses, spoken in front of thousands of people, and am currently teaching teens how they can sell online too!

Oxana Ungureanu

Oxana Ungureanu is the CEO and Founder of TRENDY PRO and BeSAFIE. With a degree in Finance and professional certifications in Project Management, Oxana is passionate about building teams and systems that allow businesses to scale to their full capacity. Oxana enjoys designing and producing games for kids. She calls it "Magic" that starts from nothing and ends with the smile of a child. She feels lucky to be responsible for thousands of smiles that enjoy TRENDY PRO products. Oxana is hoping that this book will inspire the reader to take action, find their own magic and share it with the word.

You can find Oxana's products at trendy-pro.com

Nicole Ungureanu

Nicole Ungureanu is 15 years old and the Founder and Designer of the brand, Annicko. Her first product reached over $150,000 in sales in the first eight weeks. She is an exceptional artist with a passion for fashion and design. Nicole enjoys videography and creating YouTube videos for her channel. Nicole is currently working on her own fashion brand called Annicko.com and is excited to make her dream of owning her own business a reality.

Leanne Woehlke

Leanne Woehlke, is an entrepreneur, life coach, yogi, podcast host, firewalk instructor, wife and mom. Leanne has a Master's Degree in Experimental Psychology, which opened the door to a career in Drug Development. After the birth of her daughter, she hung up her corporate suit to pursue a life of balance, focused on the people and things she loved. This sounded like pure paradise, until eleven days later, her husband was diagnosed with a rare form of cancer. The experience of his diagnosis and treatment inspired her to open EPIC YOGA in

2011 in an attempt to help others find more peace, health and balance in their lives. Leanne is host of The EPIC Journey, a top 100 ranked podcast, where she shares thoughts and lessons learned on her health and wellness entrepreneurial journey. As a Senior Leader for Tony Robbins, Leanne loves studying personal growth and transformation, and contributing to the growth of others. Leanne lives outside of Nashville, Tennessee, with her husband and daughter. When she's not on a yoga mat, you can often find her dreaming of travel adventures, paddling at the lake, or walking the family dog, Holly, up long hills.

You can connect with Leanne at:

The EPIC Journey Podcast:

https://podcasts.apple.com/us/podcast/the-epic-journey/id1485304828

https://linkedin.com/in/leanne-woehlke

https://www.facebook.com/leanne.woehlke

https://www.instagram.com/epic.yoga.life/

https://www.epicyogacenter.com

https://www.epicyogaonline.com

https://www.teachyogaonline.com

Kathryn Woehlke

Kathryn Woehlke is a 14-year-old entrepreneur, podcast host and CEO of her own company, focused on impacting other young people. Kathryn seeks to inspire, motivate, and mentor young entrepreneurs into becoming who they dream. After attending an event to teach kids about entrepreneurship, Kathryn launched her top 100 ranked podcast, The Bright Podcast. In mid-2020 Kathryn launched her course, Bright Industries, to help kids and young people create profitable companies while impacting the world. She wanted to break down the myth that you need a ton of time, cash, or experience to make a meaningful difference in the world. Kathryn's mission is to help young entrepreneurs bring their ideas to life and at the same time master the mindset and entrepreneurial essentials that will lead to a life of success and possibility. Kathryn believes that if you have a passion for something, there is a profitable company hidden beneath it. Kathryn currently lives outside Nashville, Tennessee, with her parents and pets. She enjoys traveling all over the world, playing travel volleyball, all things fashion, and hanging out with her amazing group of friends. Be sure to subscribe to The Bright Podcast:

https://podcasts.apple.com/us/podcast/the-bright-podcast/id1506355033

Jamie Wolf

Jamie Wolf, MBA, is CEO and President of Million Dollar Story Agency and Owner of Wolf Tide Publishing. Her Agency helps mission-and-success driven entrepreneurs 10X their impact and ROI by becoming published, Best Selling authors FAST while leveraging a strategic network of top influencers in your niche. If you want to make more sales and position yourself as an expert quickly - even if you are not a writer - we have a unique proprietary system that will instantly boost your credibility and sales; it's like you're getting a commercial during the Super Bowl!

Jamie has been fortunate enough to have a long and varied professional journey which includes obtaining both a Bachelor of Science and a Master's degree in Business and she's worked extensively in both science and business. In fact, she merged the two fields when she co-founded a medical tech and disease management company that got a product through FDA clearance in less than two years while raising millions of dollars. Over a lifetime of work, she's been in the role of student, employee, corporate management, consultant, tech start-up co-founder, syndicated columnist, author, publisher, and owner of a brick and mortar. What emerged from those experiences is a passion for working with success-and-mission-driven entrepreneurs to help them tell their stories and significantly grow their revenue, influence, and impact. If you've always wanted to become a published Best Selling author and get your book out to the world fast, contact her at MillionDollarStory.co! You can also listen to powerful stories filled with action items at Million Dollar PIVOT, on iTunes and other podcast sites.

Made in the USA
Las Vegas, NV
18 September 2021